HTV COOKBOOK

HTV COOKBOOK

HTV COOKBOOK

HANDY ONE-PAGE "RECIPES" FOR
100+ IRON-ON VINYL PROJECTS

BY
JENNIFERMAKER

HTV COOKBOOK

ABOUT THIS COOKBOOK

In this cookbook, you will find **recipes for applying all types of heat transfer vinyl (HTV) to as many different materials as I could think of**, as well as everything you need to know about equipment, times, temperatures, pressures, and other details to create awesome HTV projects. Think of this cookbook as your personal pre-filled HTV notebook with all the information others may spend years or decades collecting — you can even add your own notes and tips as you go along! We've done the work for you!

Are you new to heat transfer vinyl? That's okay! This cookbook will teach you all you need to know, from what heat transfer vinyl is to how to use it to create SO many different projects! Each "recipe" tells you exactly what you need and includes a step-by-step tutorial.

To learn more about the different types of vinyl, check out my **beginner-friendly ultimate guide to vinyl** over at jennifermaker.com/ultimate-guide-to-vinyl.

To learn about the must-have tools and accessories, check out jennifermaker.com/what-cricut-accessories-need.

If you have any questions about this cookbook, please head over to jennifermaker.com/cricutcrafters or email me at vip@jennifermaker.com.

Happy crafting,

Version 1.0 - September 2023 • Copyright 2023 by JenniferMaker Creative Living

All rights reserved. This book or parts thereof may not be reproduced in any form, stored in any retrieval system, or transmitted in any form by any means—electronic, mechanical, photocopy, recording, or otherwise—without prior written permission of the publisher, except as provided by United States of America copyright law.

Cricut® and Cricut Design Space® are registered trademarks of Provo Craft. Siser EasySubli® is a registered trademark of Siser. ColorSpark® is a registered trademark of The Rhinestone World, Inc. Use of them does not imply any affiliation with or endorsement by them. This is an unofficial educational resource that is not associated with Cricut®, Siser®, or The Rhinestone World®.

HTV COOKBOOK

COOKBOOK PAGES

About This Cookbook 2
What is HTV? 4
Equipment 5
Vinyl Types 7
Pressures and Temperatures 9
Cutting Tips and Tricks 11
How to Layer HTV 13

Chapter 1: Standard Color Heat Transfer Vinyl/Everyday Iron-on 14
Cotton, Polyester, Cotton/Poly Blend, Nylon, Glass, Metal, Cardstock, Felt, Burlap, Canvas, Faux Leather, Wood, Cork, Neoprene, Ceramic, Polypropylene

Chapter 2: Flex/Stretch Heat Transfer Vinyl 31
Athletic Mesh, Stretch Polyester, Spandex, Nylon, Cotton/Poly Blend, Poly/Nylon Blend, Neoprene, Siser EasyWeed Stretch

Chapter 3: Mesh Heat Transfer Vinyl 40
Burlap, Nylon, Canvas, Cotton, Cotton/Poly Blend, Polyester, Wood, Neoprene

Chapter 4: Holographic Heat Transfer Vinyl 49
Polyester, Cotton, Cotton/Poly Blend, Canvas, Faux Leather, Burlap, Cardstock, Wood, Cork, Neoprene, Ceramic

Chapter 5: Glitter Heat Transfer Vinyl 61
Cotton, Polyester, Canvas, Glass, Metal, Neoprene, Ceramic

Chapter 6: Foil Heat Transfer Vinyl 69
Polyester, Cotton, Cotton/Poly Blend, Canvas, Wood, Cork, Neoprene

Chapter 7: Patterned Heat Transfer Vinyl 77
Cotton, Polyester, Wood, Cotton/Poly Blend, Canvas, Faux Leather, Neoprene, Corkboard, Chameleon

Chapter 8: Glow-in-the-dark Heat Transfer Vinyl 87
Polyester, Cotton, Cotton/Poly Blend, Poly/Nylon Blend, Wood, Neoprene

Chapter 9: UV Color Change Heat Transfer Vinyl 94
Cotton, Cotton/Poly Blend, Polyester, Canvas, Wood, Neoprene, Burlap, Cork, Faux Leather, Nylon

Chapter 10: Puff Heat Transfer Vinyl 105
Cotton, Cotton/Poly blend, Canvas, Felt, Polyester

Chapter 11: Flocked Heat Transfer Vinyl 111
Cotton, Cotton/Poly Blend, Spandex, Felt, Polyester, Athletic Mesh

Chapter 12: Everything Else (Hacks for HTV) 118
Printable HTV Light Materials, Printable HTV Dark Materials, Colorspark, Clear HTV for Sublimation, Glitter HTV for Sublimation, Holographic HTV for Sublimation, Glow-in-the-Dark HTV for Sublimation, EasySubli

More Resources 127

HTV COOKBOOK

WHAT IS HTV?

What does HTV stand for?
HTV stands for Heat Transfer Vinyl. Iron-on vinyl refers to the same material!

How does it work?
HTV has a liner or carrier sheet covering the pretty side of the vinyl that will eventually be seen. The carrier sheet is usually clear and makes that side look shiny. The other side of the HTV looks dull and has adhesive; however, the adhesive is not sticky to the touch. To make it stick, you put the dull side on your project and apply specific heat and pressure through the carrier sheet for a set amount of time. This is called pressing! The adhesive bonds to the base material and then you can peel the carrier sheet off revealing permanent decoration!

What does it mean to peel up the carrier sheets from the HTV?
After you press HTV, you need to remove the clear carrier sheet to make sure the vinyl stuck. Just grab a corner of the sheet and peel it away from the project, but the timing depends on the project! Some recipes will say to do a "warm peel," which means the clear sheet should still be warm to the touch but NOT hot enough to burn you. Other projects need to sit a little longer for the vinyl to bond to the surface. Those are called "cool peel," so wait until the carrier sheet is totally cooled off. The correct peel can make all the difference, so always check the instructions in this book's recipes.

What is it used for? How can I use HTV?
You can use HTV to decorate SO MANY projects, that's why I love it! Clothing, accessories, home decor — indoors and out! — the possibilities are nearly endless. As long as it's made out of a compatible material and you can apply pressure and heat to the item, you can add HTV to it!

What can I put HTV on? What base materials does it work on?
I've applied HTV to lots of different materials in my craft projects! It works AH-mazingly on many fabrics, from cotton to cardstock. I love HTV's versatility! I've also used it on athletic mesh/jersey, burlap, stretched canvas, corkboard, cotton/polyester blends, faux leather, felt, glass, metal, neoprene, nylon, polyester, polyester/nylon blends, nylons, spandex, and even wood! Just make sure you pick the right kind of HTV for your project! I explain what to use in this cookbook.

So what kinds of HTV are available?
Standard HTV comes in tons of colors and patterns, but there's also special stretch HTV for athletic fabric, holographic, foil, and glitter styles for some sparkle. And there are more unusual kinds coming out all the time, like flocked and puff vinyl to add texture, or glow-in-the-dark and color-changing HTV that reacts to UV light or temperature changes! There's even HTV you can use for super special projects, like printing, sublimating, and a whole lot more.

Is HTV waterproof?
Yes! As long as you get a solid stick when you press HTV, it will hold up to water and can be used on both soft and hard surfaces. HTV on fabric items will last longest if you wait 24 hours before machine washing them and then only wash them inside out. And you can use normal soap and water on projects applied to hard materials!

HTV COOKBOOK
EQUIPMENT

You will need several pieces of equipment to complete the recipes in this cookbook. Here you will find a list of the equipment and a short description of each item. You will only need some of the equipment listed to complete any single recipe, so don't purchase any items until you know you need them! Visit jennifermaker.com/htv-project-resources for more information on equipment you need.

EQUIPMENT USED
- ☐ Cutting machine
- ☐ Heat source
- ☐ Cover sheet
- ☐ Weeding tool
- ☐ Pressing pad
- ☐ Lint roller
- ☐ Microfiber cloth
- ☐ Rubbing alcohol

OPTIONAL EQUIPMENT USED
- ☐ Pressing pillow/foam insert
- ☐ Heat-resistant gloves
- ☐ Ruler or T-shirt ruler
- ☐ Sandpaper
- ☐ Scraper
- ☐ Heat-resistant tape

A NOTE ABOUT HEAT SOURCES
Most HTV is pressed at 270°F to 350°F (132°C-177°C). If you are using a household iron or heat gun, check out the page titled "Pressures and Temperatures" to learn all about the best settings to use.

A NOTE ABOUT COVER SHEETS
A cover sheet sits on top of your heat transfer vinyl and carrier sheet to protect the base material and vinyl from the heat source. You can use parchment paper, uncoated butcher paper, Teflon sheets, and thin fabric as cover sheets. Unless otherwise specified, use whatever is available to you. For example, in Chapter 12, you will see that blowout paper is used. You can use uncoated butcher paper for this or a piece of white cardstock. Some brands of HTV suggest that you use a cover sheet, while others do not need a cover sheet. For example, Cricut Everyday Iron-on does not need one.

Cutting Machine
While you can hand-cut your own designs out of HTV, you'll have a much easier time using a cutting machine. Cricut makes many great machines, all of which I LOVE and recommend, and there are other manufacturers as well. Use what you have available.

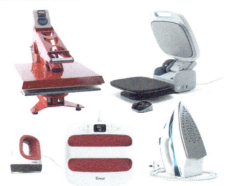

Heat Source
You'll need a heat source that can reach up to 350°F (177°C) to adhere HTV to base materials. Each recipe lists the time, temperature, and pressure for a variety of heat sources, including a traditional heat press, Autopress, EasyPress, Mini Press, and household iron. You can sometimes use a heat gun, too. There are many different types of heat sources. Use what you have available.

HTV COOKBOOK

Weeding Tool
Use a weeding tool to pull away the unwanted parts of vinyl after you cut your designs with a cutting machine.

Cover Sheet
Use uncoated butcher paper, parchment paper, or a Teflon sheet as a protective layer between your vinyl carrier sheet and heat source.

Pressing Pad
Use a pressing pad to support even pressure when pressing your vinyl to base materials. You can also use a neatly folded towel or a thick wood cutting board in a pinch.

Lint Roller
Use a lint roller with disposable sticky sheets to help remove dirt, dust, and debris from your base materials.

OPTIONAL EQUIPMENT:

Microfiber Cloth
This soft cloth leaves no lint and can remove dust and debris from certain base materials.

Rubbing Alcohol
Use rubbing alcohol, along with a microfiber cloth, to clean the surface of certain base materials, such as glass and metal.

Pressing Pillow/Foam
The pressing pillow/foam insert goes inside your base materials to create an even pressing surface. They are commonly used with materials that contain zippers and seams that could interfere with getting an even press.

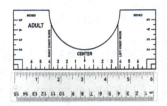

Ruler or T-Shirt Ruler
Any ruler can measure the base materials for placement of vinyl. A T-shirt ruler helps center a design on any shirt. Get my free T-shirt rulers at jennifermaker.com/t-shirt-rulers

Heat-Resistant Gloves
Use any gloves designed to protect your hands from heat to handle certain base materials that heat up very quickly. Recommended for items below 450°F/232°C.

Sandpaper
Use sandpaper to prepare the surface of wood blanks in order to allow the heat transfer vinyl to adhere properly.

Scraper
The scraper is useful for adhering the vinyl to the machine mat prior to cutting, as well as securing vinyl to wood projects.

Heat-Resistant Tape
In most cases, the carrier sheet holds your design in place during transfer. However, if needed, use heat-resistant tape to secure your design in place.

HTV COOKBOOK

INGREDIENTS: VINYL

Heat transfer vinyl comes in various types, finishes, and textures. There are many manufacturers of most types of heat transfer vinyl, so use your favorite brands. Different brands may have their own directions from the manufacturer, so use your best judgment when applying the recipes in this book. Read this section to learn about each of the varieties of HTV used in this cookbook.

STANDARD: Standard heat transfer vinyl, which is also called Everyday Iron-On vinyl, comes in many matte and glossy colors. Standard HTV can be layered and works well on polyester, cotton, cotton/polyester blends, nylon, canvas, faux leather, glass, metal, wood, corkboard, cardstock, neoprene, felt, burlap, and more. If you are using Cricut Everyday Iron-On vinyl in a single layer, you do not have to use a cover sheet.

FLEX/STRETCH: Flex/Stretch heat transfer vinyl is thinner than standard HTV and is designed to stretch and flex. It is available in solid colors and **can be layered with other Flex/Stretch HTV only.** It works well on athletic mesh/jersey material, stretch polyester, spandex, nylon, cotton/polyester blends, polyester/nylon blends, neoprene, and more.

MESH: Mesh heat transfer vinyl has very small holes patterned across it. It is available in solid colors, as well as glitter. **If layering, mesh HTV should not be layered underneath another layer of heat transfer vinyl.** Mesh HTV works well on burlap, nylon, canvas, cotton, cotton/polyester blends, polyester, wood, neoprene, and more.

HOLOGRAPHIC: Holographic heat transfer vinyl has an iridescent finish and comes in many colors. **If layering, holographic HTV should not be layered underneath another layer of heat transfer vinyl.** Holographic HTV works well on polyester, cotton, polyester/cotton blends, canvas, faux leather, burlap, cardstock, wood, corkboard, neoprene, and more.

GLITTER: Glitter heat transfer vinyl has a textured glitter finish and is available in solid colors. **If layering, glitter HTV should not be layered underneath another layer of heat transfer vinyl.** Glitter HTV works well on cotton, polyester, canvas, glass, metal, neoprene, and more.

HTV COOKBOOK

FOIL: Foil heat transfer vinyl has a bright shine and comes in solid colors. **If layering, foil HTV should not be layered underneath another layer of heat transfer vinyl.** Foil HTV works well on polyester, cotton, cotton blends, canvas, wood, corkboard, neoprene, and more.

PATTERNED: Patterned heat transfer vinyl comes in a huge variety of colors and patterns — from checkered and swirls to licensed designs. Patterned HTV works well on cotton, polyester, cotton/polyester blends, canvas, faux leather, corkboard, neoprene, wood, and more.

GLOW-IN-THE-DARK: Glow-in-the-dark heat transfer vinyl has a light green, yellow, blue, pink, or orange appearance when uncharged, and glows with bright luminescence in the dark after it is charged in direct light. Glow-in-the-dark HTV works well on cotton, cotton blends, polyester, polyester/nylon blends, wood, neoprene, and more.

UV COLOR CHANGE: UV color change heat transfer vinyl appears matte white at first but changes color when exposed to UV light, such as sunlight. UV color change HTV works well on cotton, polyester, cotton/polyester blends, canvas, wood, neoprene, burlap, corkboard, faux leather, nylon, and more.

PUFF: Puff heat transfer vinyl comes flat so it can be cut, and puffs up when heat and heavy pressure is applied. Very heavy pressure is necessary to create a good puff effect. It comes in solid colors. **If layering, it should not be layered underneath another layer of heat transfer vinyl.** Puff HTV works well on cotton, cotton blends, polyester, canvas, and more.

FLOCKED: Flocked heat transfer vinyl has a soft, velvety texture and comes in solid colors. **If layering, flocked HTV should not be layered underneath another layer of heat transfer vinyl.** Flocked HTV works well on cotton, polyester, cotton/polyester blends, spandex, linen, athletic mesh/jersey, and more.

PRINTABLE HEAT TRANSFER PAPER: Printable heat transfer paper is not actually vinyl, though it is sometimes called printable HTV. This paper accepts regular inkjet printer ink, and the design is usually printed as one full-color piece. Printable heat transfer paper works well on cotton, polyester, cotton/polyester blends, and nylon.

HTV COOKBOOK

PRESSURES AND TEMPERATURES

HTV needs more than just heat and time to stick well to a surface. It needs pressure, too! Read below to learn all about pressure, then read the next page to learn about temperature and how to combine pressure and temperature for successful projects.

PRESSURE

Pressure is weight applied to your base material and vinyl from the heat press and/or your own body strength. Throughout the cookbook, you will see three pressure settings: 30 psi (light), 40 psi (medium), and 50 psi (firm). "PSI" stands for pounds per square inch. The amount of pressure you use depends on the type of vinyl and the base material you are using. The right amount of pressure allows the heat to distribute evenly across the base material. If your pressure is too high, it can overheat and even scorch the vinyl and the material. If it is too low, the adhesive on the vinyl will not adhere completely to the base material and will easily peel off.

One more thing — it's not ideal to press HTV on an ironing board, but rather a sturdy heat-resistant surface like a wooden kitchen table or wooden desk. Don't press on top of a glass surface.

Here's how to press at each pressure setting:

Light Pressure
- **Traditional Heat Press:** Set the pressure to 30 psi.
- **AutoPress:** The AutoPress automatically adjusts to find the correct pressure setting!
- **EasyPress, MiniPress, & Household Iron:** Use the press or iron on a waist-high table for best results. Use one hand on the press or iron and apply approximately 5-10 pounds of body weight, which means you should be pressing your hand down gently. The EasyPresses weigh between 3.3 and 8.6 pounds, so the heavier your press is, the less pressure you need to manually apply. If the vinyl peels up when you pull the cover sheet, you are not using enough pressure.

Medium Pressure
- **Traditional Heat Press:** Set the pressure to 40 psi.
- **AutoPress:** The AutoPress automatically adjusts to find the correct pressure setting!
- **EasyPress, MiniPress, & Household Iron:** Use the press or iron on a waist-high table for best results. Use one hand on the press or iron and apply approximately 10-15 pounds of body weight, which means you should be pressing your hand down a little more firmly than when using a light pressure setting. The EasyPresses weigh between 3.3 and 8.6 pounds, so the heavier your press is, the less pressure you need to manually apply.

Firm Pressure
- **Traditional Heat Press:** Set the pressure to 50 psi.
- **AutoPress:** The AutoPress automatically adjusts to find the correct pressure setting!
- **EasyPress, MiniPress, & Household Iron:** Use the press or iron on a waist-high table for best results. Use two hands on the press or iron and apply 15-20 pounds of body weight, which means you should use some of your arm strength to push down. The EasyPresses weigh between 3.3 and 8.6 pounds, so the heavier your press is, the less pressure you need to manually apply. Contrary to popular belief, you do not need the weave or texture of your fabric to be seen through the HTV to indicate a good press, and in some cases, it's not even possible (source: Siser). Check out https://www.siserna.com/sisers-top-10-htv-tip-tricks-pt-2 for more information.

HTV COOKBOOK

TEMPERATURE

Temperature refers to how hot your heat source should be. The correct temperature is SO important because it helps make sure that the adhesive on the vinyl sticks well to the base material. A temperature setting that is too high can cause scorching of the vinyl or material, but a temperature setting that is too low can cause the vinyl to peel up.

HOW THE PRESSURE AND TEMPERATURE SETTINGS APPEAR IN THE RECIPES

Near the bottom of each recipe, you will find a chart with the temperature, pressure, and time needed to make sure the vinyl sticks to the base material. Please note that these times and temperatures can vary with your specific materials and the type of press being used, so always check the instructions that come with your materials. Any additional details about the pre-pressing temperatures and times will be within the recipe steps.

Here is an example of what the charts on each recipe page look like. I have also included a column for you to write down your favorite settings!

your favorite settings

Traditional Heat Press	AutoPress	EasyPress	Mini Press	
305°F / 151°C	305°F / 151°C	305°F / 151°C	Medium	
20 seconds	20 seconds	20 seconds	25 seconds	
50 psi (Firm pressure)	Auto pressure	Firm pressure	Firm pressure	

HOUSEHOLD IRON

Unlike a heat press, you usually can't set the exact temperature on your household iron. Instead, you'll pick a fabric setting depending on the type of heat transfer vinyl you are using and the base material of your blank. You can use the "linen" setting most of the time, but you should always do a test cut and application before using the iron on your actual project, just in case! For a tutorial on how to use a household iron to apply heat transfer vinyl, check out jennifermaker.com/how-to-iron-on-cricut-vinyl.

HEAT GUN

Sometimes, a flat heat press just doesn't work well for applying heat transfer vinyl to blanks with curved surfaces, such as tumblers, mugs, and cups. In these cases, a heat gun can be carefully used to adhere heat transfer vinyl to the surface of the blank. To do this, place the blank on a dishtowel. Most heat guns have settings that start too high for heat transfer vinyl, so if your heat gun has a "Low" setting, use that. Bring the heat gun close to the carrier sheet on top of the vinyl and the surface of the blank (a little less an inch away), and heat each section for the time recommended in each recipe. If you get the heat gun too close to the vinyl or spend too long on a section, the vinyl can melt. After heating each section, use a microfiber cloth to press down on the carrier sheet and vinyl. Don't use your bare hands, because you can get burned. Safety is so important! Using the microfiber cloth to firmly press down is necessary to make sure the vinyl sticks to the blank. Once the blank and vinyl have cooled, peel the carrier sheet away. If any pieces of vinyl peel up, put the carrier sheet back in place and use a little more heat and pressure.

HTV COOKBOOK

CUTTING TIPS & TRICKS

Have you created an awesome design in your software and are now ready to cut your heat transfer vinyl? Remember these important tips and tricks on this page and the next when it's time to cut your vinyl. These can help prevent hiccups and frustration along the way!

REMEMBER TO MIRROR YOUR DESIGN
For almost every type of heat transfer vinyl, you will need to mirror your design before cutting it. This means reversing your design so it appears backward when it cuts. This is super important if your design has any words or phrases. Remember to do this before you send your design to the cutting machine, and it will save you a lot of wasted vinyl, time, and frustration.

MAKE A WEEDING BOX OR OFFSET
Before you send your design to your cutting machine, use your cutting machine software to draw a box around your design, or make .25 inch offset (if your design software has this feature). This is a great trick for designs with words and phrases or small and intricate details. Once the design is cut, you can weed your design much more quickly and in smaller sections. See how at jennifermaker.com/reverse-weed-vinyl.

CHOOSE THE RIGHT CUT SETTING
Not all heat transfer vinyl has the same cut setting. It is important that you use the correct setting for the type of vinyl you are cutting. For example, glitter HTV will not cut well using the standard HTV setting because it is much thicker and has a different texture than standard HTV.

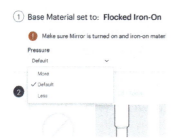

CHOOSE THE RIGHT PRESSURE SETTING
Just like you must choose the right cut setting for your vinyl, you also need to use the right pressure setting. For thicker heat transfer vinyl, such as glitter and flock, I like to use the "more pressure" setting rather than the default pressure setting. This helps make sure that your cutting machine will cut through the vinyl entirely the first time!

HTV COOKBOOK

MAKE SURE THE CARRIER SHEET IS AGAINST THE MAT
When you place your vinyl on a machine mat, the shiny plastic carrier sheet must go face down against the machine mat. If the carrier sheet is placed face up on the mat, your machine will cut it instead of the vinyl. For more information on this, visit my blog post at jennifermaker.com/which-side.

USE A BRAYER AND SCRAPER TO ADHERE VINYL TO THE MAT
Once you've used your hands to smooth the vinyl down on a machine mat, use a brayer to firmly secure it. If you need to, use a scraper to carefully work out any bubbles and creases. This will reduce the chances of your cutting machine causing any rips, tears, or missed areas as it is cutting your design.

KEEP YOUR BLADE CLEAN
If your cutting machine starts tearing or ripping your vinyl, or misses parts that should have been cut, it might be time to check your blade. Remove the blade housing from your cutting machine and carefully press the blade 40 to 50 times into a tightly crumpled aluminum foil ball. This helps clean any residue or debris off the blade. For more information, visit my blog post at jennifermaker.com/cricut-blades-cutting-tips.

USE A BRIGHT LIGHT SOURCE FOR INTRICATE WEEDING
If you have intricate cuts or are using a heat transfer vinyl that makes it challenging to see cut lines for weeding, like glitter HTV, use a lightbox, lightpad, or Cricut Brightpad. Just lay your vinyl on top and start weeding! For more information on the Cricut BrightPad and BrightPad Go, visit my blog post at jennifermaker.com/cricut-brightpad.

REMOVE THE MAT FROM THE VINYL
When your cutting machine has finished cutting your vinyl, peel the mat away from the vinyl rather than pull the vinyl off the mat. Simply flip the mat over so the vinyl is against your work surface, then slowly peel the mat away while placing your hand on the vinyl to keep it flat. It is SO much easier to work with flat vinyl rather than vinyl that has curled.

HOW TO LAYER HTV

Does your design have more than one color of vinyl? If so, you will need to layer the vinyl on your base material. Layering can sound scary, but it's actually pretty easy once you know how to do it! However, remember that not all types of HTV can be layered. See pages 7 and 8 for which types of vinyl you can layer. Below are step-by-step instructions for how to layer heat transfer vinyl.

STEP ONE
Pre-heat your base material. Use a cover sheet if necessary. Allow it to cool for at least 30 seconds before continuing.

STEP TWO
Lay all of your vinyl pieces out to ensure you have them all. Then, put the layers of your design together to ensure it fits together the way you expect. Don't worry, this won't hurt your design! You're just testing the look. You can lift the layers away when you're ready to move on.

STEP THREE
Place the bottom layer of vinyl on your base material. Place a cover sheet on top if necessary. Press for 3 to 5 seconds, which is just long enough to tack it down. Remove any cover sheet as well as the carrier sheet while still warm. Allow the vinyl to cool for at least 30 seconds. Repeat this step for each layer except the very top one. Use a cover sheet each time to make sure no parts of vinyl are directly exposed to the heat source.

STEP FOUR
Place the top and final layer on your base material, making sure to align it properly according to the other layers. Place a cover sheet on top if necessary. Press for a bit longer, at least 10 seconds. You may need to press for a little bit longer, depending on your base material. Remove any cover sheet as well as the carrier sheet while still warm. You're done! Enjoy your beautiful layered vinyl project!

For more information on layering heat transfer vinyl, visit my blog posts listed below!
- jennifermaker.com/layer-iron-on-vinyl-shirt
- jennifermaker.com/how-to-layer-vinyl-on-a-shirt
- jennifermaker.com/layer-iron-on-vinyl-cricut-tote-bag

CHAPTER 1
STANDARD HTV

STANDARD HTV

COTTON

T-Shirt, blanket, burp cloth, dress, hoodie, infant bodysuit, long-sleeved shirt, lounge pants, pajamas, pillowcase, plushie, polo shirt, shorts, sweatshirt, tank top

Items made from 100% cotton work well for heat transfer vinyl. The versatility of the material makes it appropriate for a variety of uses from household items to clothing.

INGREDIENTS
- ☐ Standard heat transfer vinyl
- ☐ Base material, such as 100% cotton T-shirt
- ☐ Cover sheet

EQUIPMENT
- ☐ Lint roller
- ☐ Weeding tool
- ☐ Flat heat source such as a heat press
- ☐ (Optional) T-shirt ruler for placement help
- ☐ (Optional) Pillow or foam insert

PREPARATION

Start with a new cotton item, such as a T-shirt, for the best results. No need to pre-wash, but if you do, avoid fabric softener. Use a lint roller to remove any loose fibers or dust from the T-shirt.

Pre-heat your flat heat press to the temperature shown in chart below.

Place the vinyl with the carrier sheet side facing down on a machine mat and then use your cutting machine to **cut your desired pattern out of the vinyl. Weed as necessary** to remove any excess vinyl from the design.

Place your T-shirt on top of the pressing pad.

If you're pressing a shirt, fold the shirt in half lengthwise so both sides match up, then **press for 5 seconds** — this both pre-heats the fabric to remove moisture and gives you a straight vertical crease for alignment.

Unfold the T-shirt. Optionally, slide a pressing pillow or foam insert inside the T-shirt to provide additional support.

Place the vinyl on the T-shirt with the carrier sheet facing up and the sticky side facing down, lining up the center of your design with your shirt's center crease. Cover with a cover sheet.

Press according to the chart below.

When the carrier sheet is cool to the touch, **slowly peel it away to reveal your design.** If your vinyl peels away from the T-shirt, carefully replace carrier sheet and apply a little more heat and pressure.

Stack (top to bottom): heat source, cover sheet, HTV with carrier sheet side up, cotton, pillow or foam*, pressing pad, work surface. **COOL PEEL**

optional

COOK TIMES
Here are typical times you can use as a starting point. Always check the manufacturer's instructions for time and temperature, when available.

your favorite settings

Traditional Heat Press	AutoPress	EasyPress	Mini Press	
305°F / 152°C	315°F / 157°C	315°F / 157°C	Medium	
15 seconds	40 seconds	30 seconds	25 seconds	
40 psi (Medium pressure)	Auto pressure	Firm pressure	Firm pressure	

TIPS & TRICKS
- ✓ Remember to mirror your design if it contains words or phrases.
- ✗ Do not wash your item for at least 24 hours after applying the HTV. If you wash a garment, turn it inside out first.

STANDARD HTV

POLYESTER

T-shirt, backpack, blanket, dress, hoodie, infant bodysuit, long-sleeved shirt, lounge pants, pajamas, pillowcase, plushie, polo shirt, shorts, tank top

Polyester is a blend of synthetic materials and is one of the most commonly used materials for textiles. Heat transfer vinyl is easily applied with low heat and medium to firm pressure.

INGREDIENTS
- ☐ Standard heat transfer vinyl
- ☐ Base material, such as polyester T-shirt
- ☐ Cover sheet

EQUIPMENT
- ☐ Weeding tool
- ☐ Lint roller
- ☐ Flat heat source such as a heat press
- ☐ (Optional) Pillow or foam insert
- ☐ (Optional) T-shirt ruler for placement help

PREPARATION

Start with a new polyester item, such as a shirt, for the best results. No need to pre-wash, but if you do, avoid fabric softener.

Pre-heat your flat heat press to the temperature listed below.

Place the vinyl with the carrier sheet side facing down on a machine mat and then use your cutting machine to **cut your desired pattern out of the vinyl. Weed as necessary** to remove any excess vinyl from the design.

Place your shirt on top of the pressing pad. Use a lint roller to remove dust or loose fibers on the shirt. **If you're pressing a shirt, fold the shirt in half lengthwise** so both sides match up, then **press for 5 seconds** — this both pre-heats the shirt to remove moisture and gives you a straight vertical crease for alignment.

Unfold the shirt. Optionally, slide a pressing pillow or foam insert inside the shirt to provide additional support.

Place the vinyl on the T-shirt with the carrier sheet facing up, lining up the center of your design with your shirt's center crease.

Place a cover sheet over the carrier sheet.

Press according to the chart below.

Flip the shirt over and apply additional heat and pressure for 15 seconds to the back side of the design.

Once the carrier sheet is cool to the touch, **slowly peel it away.**

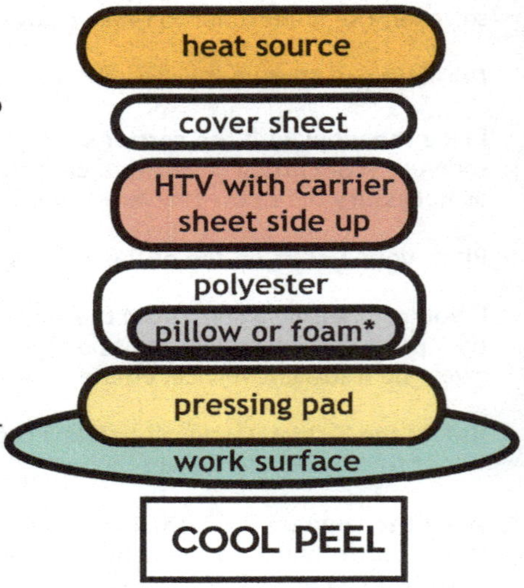

Stack (top to bottom):
- heat source
- cover sheet
- HTV with carrier sheet side up
- polyester
- pillow or foam*
- pressing pad
- work surface

COOL PEEL

*optional

COOK TIMES

Here are typical times you can use as a starting point. Always check the manufacturer's instructions for time and temperature, when available.

your favorite settings

Traditional Heat Press	AutoPress	EasyPress	Mini Press	
270°F / 132°C	315°F / 157°C	315°F / 157°C	Medium	
15 seconds	30 seconds	30 seconds	25 seconds	
40 psi (Medium pressure)	Auto pressure	Firm pressure	Firm pressure	

TIPS & TRICKS
- ✓ Remember to mirror your design if it contains words or phrases.
- ✓ For an additional tutorial on this recipe, check out jennifermaker.com/DIY-custom-t-shirts
- ✗ Do not wash your item for at least 24 hours after applying the HTV. If you wash a garment, turn it inside out first.

STANDARD HTV

COTTON/POLY BLEND

T-shirt, blanket, burp cloth, dress, hoodie, infant bodysuit, long-sleeved shirt, lounge pants, pajamas, pillowcase, plushie, polo shirt, shorts, sweatshirt, tank top

Cotton blends, often found as 50/50 cotton/polyester, of any color are a popular base material for standard heat transfer vinyl. The vinyl can be applied anywhere on the shirt.

INGREDIENTS
- ☐ Standard heat transfer vinyl
- ☐ Base material, such as cotton blend T-shirt
- ☐ Cover sheet

EQUIPMENT
- ☐ Lint roller
- ☐ Weeding tool
- ☐ Flat heat source such as a heat press
- ☐ (Optional) T-shirt ruler for placement help
- ☐ (Optional) Pillow or foam insert

PREPARATION

Start with a new cotton/polyester blend item, such as a shirt, for the best results. No need to pre-wash, but if you do, avoid fabric softener.

Pre-heat your flat heat press to the temperature shown in chart below.

Place the vinyl with the carrier sheet side facing down on a machine mat and then use your cutting machine to **cut your desired pattern out of the vinyl. Weed as necessary** to remove any excess vinyl from the design.

Use a lint roller to remove any dust or fibers from the shirt.

If you're pressing a shirt, fold the shirt in half lengthwise so both sides match up, then **press for 5 seconds** — this both pre-heats the shirt to remove moisture and gives you a straight vertical crease for alignment.

Unfold the shirt and lay it flat. Optionally, slide a pressing pillow inside the shirt to provide additional support.

Place the vinyl on the T-shirt with the carrier sheet facing up and the sticky side facing down, lining up the center of your design with your shirt's center crease.

Cover the carrier sheet and vinyl with a cover sheet to help avoid overheating the vinyl.

Press according to the chart below.

Let cool, then slowly peel away the carrier sheet.

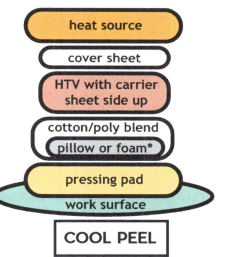

COOL PEEL

optional

COOK TIMES

Here are typical times you can use as a starting point. Always check the manufacturer's instructions for time and temperature, when available.

your favorite settings

Traditional Heat Press	AutoPress	EasyPress	Mini Press	
315°F / 157°C	315°F / 157°C	315°F / 157°C	Medium	
30 seconds	30 seconds	30 seconds	40 seconds	
50 psi (firm pressure)	Auto pressure	Firm pressure	Firm pressure	

TIPS & TRICKS
- ✓ Remember to mirror your design if it contains words or phrases.
- ✗ Do not wash your item for at least 24 hours after applying the HTV. If you wash a garment, turn it inside out first.

STANDARD HTV

NYLON

Drawstring bag, activewear, backpack, poncho, puff vest, swimwear, tech accessory bag, umbrella, windbreaker

Nylon is a synthetic fabric with a variety of uses. It can melt or burn, so extra care is needed when applying heat transfer vinyl.

INGREDIENTS
- ☐ Standard heat transfer vinyl
- ☐ Base material, such as drawstring bag
- ☐ Cover sheet

EQUIPMENT
- ☐ Lint roller
- ☐ Weeding tool
- ☐ Flat heat source such as a heat press
- ☐ (Optional) Ruler for placement help
- ☐ (Optional) Pillow or foam for inside the bag

PREPARATION

Start with a new nylon item, such as a drawstring bag, for the best results. No need to pre-wash, but if you do, avoid fabric softener.

Pre-heat your flat heat press to the temperature shown in chart below.

Place the vinyl with the carrier sheet side facing down on a machine mat and then use your cutting machine to **cut your desired pattern out of the vinyl. Weed as necessary** to remove any excess vinyl from the design.

Use a lint roller to remove any dust or fibers from the nylon.

Optionally, slide a pressing pillow or foam insert inside the nylon to provide additional support and reduce wrinkling.

Place a cover sheet on top of the nylon. **Pre-heat the nylon for 5 seconds. Remove** the cover sheet.

Place the vinyl on the nylon with the carrier sheet facing up.

Cover the carrier sheet and vinyl with a cover sheet to help avoid overheating the vinyl and melting the nylon base.

Press according to the chart below.

Let cool, then **slowly peel away the carrier sheet.** If the vinyl peels away from the nylon, carefully replace the carrier sheet and apply a little more heat and pressure for a short amount of time.

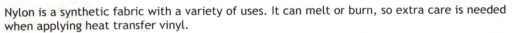

Stack order (top to bottom): heat source, cover sheet, HTV with carrier sheet side up, nylon, pillow or foam*, pressing pad, work surface.

COOL PEEL

optional

COOK TIMES

Here are typical times you can use as a starting point. Always check the manufacturer's instructions for time and temperature, when available.

your favorite settings

Traditional Heat Press	AutoPress	EasyPress	Mini Press	
280°F / 138°C	280°F / 138°C	280°F / 138°C	Low	
30 seconds	30 seconds	30 seconds	45 seconds	
50 psi (firm pressure)	Auto pressure	Firm pressure	Firm pressure	

TIPS & TRICKS

✓ Remember to mirror your design if it contains words or phrases.
✓ Be sure to use a cover sheet to avoid accidentally burning or melting the nylon with the heat press.
✗ Do not wash your item for at least 24 hours after applying the HTV. If you wash a garment, turn it inside out first.

STANDARD HTV

GLASS

Glass block, candle holder, drinking glass, pane, panel, plaque, vase

Since glass is a conductor of heat, it is an easy material to apply heat transfer vinyl to. You can apply to a variety of glass surfaces using caution as it does heat quickly and can be fragile.

INGREDIENTS
☐ Standard heat transfer vinyl
☐ Base material, such as glass block
☐ Cover sheet

EQUIPMENT
☐ Microfiber cloth
☐ Rubbing alcohol
☐ Weeding tool
☐ Flat heat source such as a heat press
☐ (Optional) Ruler for placement help

PREPARATION

Start with a new glass item, such as a glass block, for the best results.

Pre-heat your flat heat press to the temperature shown in chart below.

Use a microfiber cloth and rubbing alcohol to clean the face of your glass. Let dry completely.

Place the vinyl with the carrier sheet side facing down on a machine mat and then use your cutting machine to **cut your desired pattern out of the vinyl. Weed as necessary** to remove any excess vinyl from the design.

Place the vinyl on the glass with the carrier sheet facing up.

Cover the carrier sheet and vinyl with a cover sheet to help avoid overheating the vinyl.

Press according to the chart below.

Let cool, then **slowly peel away the carrier sheet.** If the vinyl peels away from the glass, carefully replace the carrier sheet and apply a little more heat and pressure for a short amount of time.

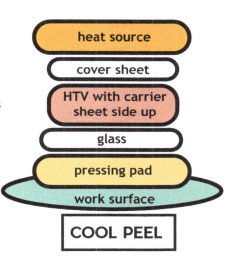

COOK TIMES

Here are typical times you can use as a starting point. Always check the manufacturer's instructions for time and temperature, when available.

your favorite settings

Traditional Heat Press	AutoPress	EasyPress	Mini Press	
315°F / 157°C	315°F / 157°C	315°F / 157°C	Medium	
15 seconds	15 seconds	15 seconds	15 seconds	
30 psi (light pressure)	Auto pressure	Light pressure	Light pressure	

TIPS & TRICKS
✓ If your glass blank has a curved surface, such as a vase or drinking glass, use a Mini Press to work around the shape of the blank. You cannot press a curved glass blank in a flat heating press.
✓ Remember to mirror your design if it contains words or phrases.
✗ Do not apply excess pressure or else you risk breaking the glass.

STANDARD HTV

METAL

Metal sign, baking tray, bin, bucket, keychain, license plate, license plate cover, lunchbox, sheet metal, tumbler

Heat transfer vinyl will adhere to most metal surfaces. Pay particular attention to heat safety when applying as metal is a conductor of heat.

INGREDIENTS
☐ Standard heat transfer vinyl
☐ Base material, such as metal sign
☐ Cover sheet

EQUIPMENT
☐ Microfiber cloth
☐ Rubbing alcohol
☐ Weeding tool
☐ Flat heat source such as a heat press
☐ Heat-resistant gloves
☐ (Optional) Ruler for placement help

PREPARATION

Start with a new metal item, such as a metal sign, for the best results.

Pre-heat your flat heat press to the temperature shown in chart below.

Use a microfiber cloth and rubbing alcohol to clean the face of your metal. Let dry completely.

Place the vinyl with the carrier sheet side facing down on a machine mat and then use your cutting machine to **cut your desired pattern out of the vinyl. Weed as necessary** to remove any excess vinyl from the design.

Align your vinyl design with the **shiny side face down on the metal.** You want the **clear plastic carrier sheet to be on the top-facing** side of the vinyl.

Place the vinyl on the metal with the carrier sheet facing up.

Press according to the chart below, using heat-resistant gloves to protect your hand from the metal, which will get hot quickly.

Let cool slightly, then **slowly peel away the carrier sheet.** If the vinyl peels away from the metal, carefully replace the carrier sheet and apply a little more heat and pressure for a short amount of time.

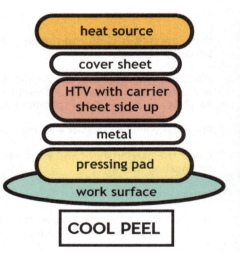

COOL PEEL

COOK TIMES
Here are typical times you can use as a starting point. Always check the manufacturer's instructions for time and temperature, when available.

your favorite settings

Traditional Heat Press	AutoPress	EasyPress	Mini Press	
300°F / 149°C	300°F / 149°C	300°F / 149°C	Medium	
15 seconds	15 seconds	15 seconds	20 seconds	
50 psi (Firm pressure)	Auto pressure	Firm pressure	Firm pressure	

TIPS & TRICKS
✓ If your metal blank has a curved surface, such as a tumbler, use a Mini Press to work around the shape of the blank. You cannot press a curved metal blank in a flat heating press.
✓ Metal heats up quickly, so use heat-resistant gloves, oven mitts, or a towel to handle it after pressing.
✗ Cookwear that has HTV application is no longer safe for cooking, these items are for display only.
✗ Do not wash your item for at least 24 hours after applying the HTV.

STANDARD HTV

CARDSTOCK

Cardstock card, cardboard, cardstock, notebook cover, notecard

Cardstock comes in almost every color, pattern, and finish you can imagine. It is available both in solid core and white core. It is available is several weights and sizes.

INGREDIENTS
☐ Standard heat transfer vinyl
☐ Base material, such as cardstock sheet
☐ Cover sheet

EQUIPMENT
☐ Lint roller
☐ Weeding tool
☐ Flat heat source such as a heat press
☐ Hard surface such as a wood cutting board or table
☐ (Optional) Ruler for placement help

PREPARATION

Start with a new sheet of cardstock for the best results.

Pre-heat your flat heat press to the temperature shown in chart below.

Place the vinyl with the carrier sheet side facing down on a machine mat and then use your cutting machine to **cut your desired pattern out of the vinyl. Weed as necessary** to remove any excess vinyl from the design.

Gently **use the lint roller** to clean any dust or debris from the face of the cardstockv.

Place the cardstock on a hard surface, such as a wood cutting board or table. Place a cover sheet over the cardstock and **pre-press for 5 seconds. Remove** the cover sheet.

Place the vinyl on the cardstock with the carrier sheet facing up.

Cover the carrier sheet and vinyl with a cover sheet to help avoid overheating the vinyl or scorching the cardstock.

Press according to the chart below. Make sure you are pressing on a hard surface so the cardstock does not warp.

Slowly peel away the carrier sheet after it is cool to the touch. If the vinyl peels away from the cardstock, carefully replace the carrier sheet and apply a little more heat and pressure for a short amount of time.

Stack (top to bottom):
- heat source
- cover sheet
- HTV with carrier sheet side up
- cardstock
- hard pressing surface
- work surface

COOL PEEL

COOK TIMES
Here are typical times you can use as a starting point. Always check the manufacturer's instructions for time and temperature, when available.

your favorite settings

Traditional Heat Press	AutoPress	EasyPress	Mini Press	
280°F / 138°C	280°F / 138°C	280°F / 138°C	Low	
20 seconds	15 seconds	30 seconds	25 seconds	
50 psi (Firm pressure)	Auto pressure	Firm pressure	Firm pressure	

TIPS & TRICKS
✓ Remember to mirror your design if it contains words or phrases.
✓ Due to the heat, the cardstock may start to curl. Lay the cardstock card under a heavy book to flatten it.

STANDARD HTV

FELT

Bunting, bag, basket, flowers, home decor, lamp shade, mobile, ornament, pillow, placemat, sleep mask, travel organizer

Felt is a very versatile fabric that is often used for accessories and decor. It is available in a wide variety of colors, prints, and thicknesses, as well as pre-stiffened or soft.

INGREDIENTS
☐ Standard heat transfer vinyl
☐ Base material, such as felt bunting piece
☐ Cover sheet

EQUIPMENT
☐ Lint roller
☐ Weeding tool
☐ Flat heat source such as a heat press
☐ (Optional) Ruler for placement help

PREPARATION

Start with a new felt item, such as bunting, for the best results.

Pre-heat your flat heat press to the temperature shown in chart below.

Place the vinyl with the carrier sheet side facing down on a machine mat and then use your cutting machine to **cut your desired pattern out of the vinyl. Weed as necessary** to remove any excess vinyl from the design.

Use the lint roller to clean away any dust or debris from the face of the bunting piece.

Pre-press the felt for 5 seconds to remove any moisture.

Place the vinyl on the bunting with the carrier sheet facing up.

Cover the carrier sheet and vinyl with a cover sheet to help avoid overheating the vinyl.

Press according to the chart below.

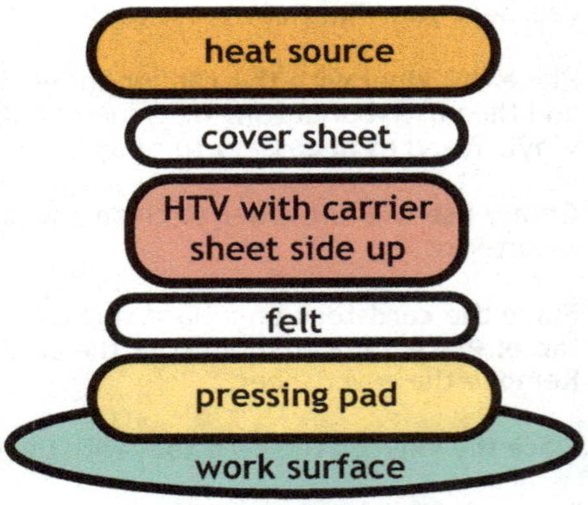

Let cool slightly, then **slowly peel away the carrier sheet after it is cool to the touch.** If the vinyl peels away from the bunting, carefully replace the carrier sheet and apply a little more heat and pressure for a short amount of time.

Stack (top to bottom): heat source / cover sheet / HTV with carrier sheet side up / felt / pressing pad / work surface

COOL PEEL

COOK TIMES
Here are typical times you can use as a starting point. Always check the manufacturer's instructions for time and temperature, when available.

your favorite settings

Traditional Heat Press	AutoPress	EasyPress	Mini Press	
280°F / 138°C	280°F / 138°C	280°F / 138°C	Low	
20 seconds	15 seconds	30 seconds	30 seconds	
50 psi (Firm pressure)	Auto pressure	Firm pressure	Firm pressure	

TIPS & TRICKS
✓ Remember to mirror your design if it contains words or phrases.
✓ Press one piece of bunting at a time.
✓ It is easier to press the heat transfer vinyl on each bunting piece before sewing or stringing them together.

STANDARD HTV

BURLAP

Wine bag, bag, banner, bunting, garden flag, pillowcase, table runner, wreath

Burlap is a material made of plant fibers. Natural burlap comes in shades of brown, but it can be dyed any color. Burlap fabric is textured and can be tightly or loosely woven.

INGREDIENTS
☐ Standard heat transfer vinyl
☐ Base material, such as burlap wine bag
☐ Cover sheet

EQUIPMENT
☐ Lint roller
☐ Weeding tool
☐ Flat heat source such as a heat press
☐ (Optional) Ruler for placement help

PREPARATION

Start with a new burlap item, such as a wine bag, for the best results.

Pre-heat your flat heat press to the temperature shown in chart below.

Place the vinyl with the carrier sheet side facing down on a machine mat and then use your cutting machine to **cut your desired pattern out of the vinyl. Weed as necessary** to remove any excess vinyl from the design.

Use the lint roller to clean any dust, debris, or loose fibers on the burlap.

Lay the burlap flat, with the seams at each side.

Pre-press the burlap for 5 seconds to eliminate moisture.

Place the vinyl on the burlap with the carrier sheet facing up.

Cover the carrier sheet and vinyl with a cover sheet to help avoid overheating the vinyl.

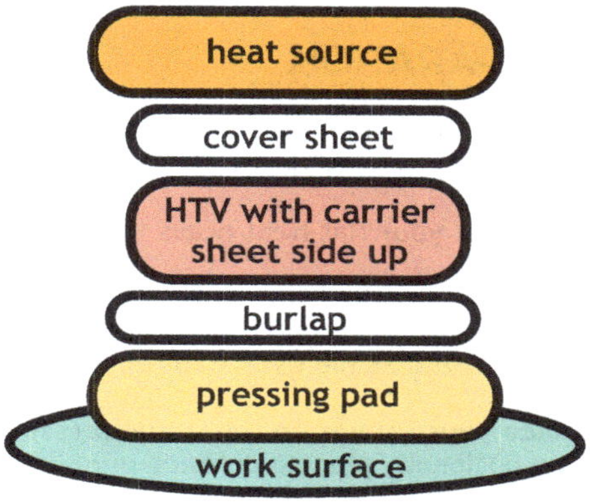

Press according to the chart below.

Let cool slightly, then **slowly peel away the carrier sheet once cool to the touch.** If the vinyl peels away from the burlap, carefully replace the carrier sheet and apply a little more heat and pressure for a short amount of time.

Repeat steps to apply vinyl to the other side, if desired.

COOK TIMES
Here are typical times you can use as a starting point. Always check the manufacturer's instructions for time and temperature, when available.

your favorite settings

Traditional Heat Press	AutoPress	EasyPress	Mini Press	
305°F / 152°C	305°F / 152°C	305°F / 152°C	Medium	
25 seconds	20 seconds	30 seconds	30 sec then flip +15 sec	
50 psi (Firm pressure)	Auto pressure	Firm pressure	Firm pressure	

TIPS & TRICKS
✓ Remember to mirror your design if it contains words or phrases.
✓ Wait until the bag has cooled completely before inserting a wine bottle.

STANDARD HTV

CANVAS

Art canvas, backdrop, cooler, flag, reverse art canvas, placemat, sail, shoes, tent, tote bag

Make sure your canvas is made of polyester or cotton and does not have any plastic components, which can melt. Plain canvas is usually cream to tan, but can be dyed any color. Canvas fabric can be very smooth or more roughly textured.

INGREDIENTS
- ☐ Standard heat transfer vinyl
- ☐ Base material, such as cotton canvas
- ☐ Cover sheet

EQUIPMENT
- ☐ Lint roller
- ☐ Weeding tool
- ☐ Flat heat source such as a heat press
- ☐ (Optional) Ruler for placement help
- ☐ (Optional) Pressing pillow or foam

PREPARATION

Start with blank canvas item, such as a stretched canvas. Choose your size based on your HTV design.

Pre-heat your flat heat press to the temperature shown in chart below.

Place the vinyl with the carrier sheet side facing down on a machine mat and then use your cutting machine to **cut your desired pattern out of the vinyl. Weed as necessary** to remove any excess vinyl from the design.

Place your canvas on top of the pressing pad. If your canvas is framed, you can optionally place a pressing pillow or foam underneath it to help provide a flat, stable surface. **Pre-heat your canvas for 5 seconds.**

Place the vinyl on the canvas with the carrier sheet facing up.

Cover the carrier sheet with a cover sheet to help avoid overheating or scorching the vinyl.

Press according to the chart below.

Once you have applied the appropriate amount of heat and pressure, allow your item to cool before you **slowly peel away your carrier sheet.**

If your vinyl peels away from the canvas, carefully replace carrier sheet and apply a little more heat and pressure.

Layers (top to bottom): heat source / cover sheet / HTV with carrier sheet side up / canvas / pressing pad / work surface

COOL PEEL

COOK TIMES
Here are typical times you can use as a starting point. Always check the manufacturer's instructions for time and temperature, when available.

Traditional Heat Press	AutoPress	EasyPress	Mini Press	your favorite settings
305°F / 152°C	340°F / 171°C	340°F / 171°C	Medium	
45-60 seconds	20 seconds	30 seconds	25 seconds	
40 psi (Medium pressure)	Auto pressure	Firm pressure	Firm pressure	

TIPS & TRICKS
- ✓ Remember to mirror your design if it contains words or phrases.
- ✗ Do not wash your item for at least 24 hours after applying the HTV. If you wash a bag, turn it inside out first.
- ✓ Check out the reverse canvas art tutorial here jennifermaker.com/reverse-canvas-project-coffee-bar-art

STANDARD HTV

FAUX LEATHER

Tote bag, baggage tag, bookmark, cosmetic bag, earrings, journal cover, notebook, wallet

Faux leather is a synthetic plastic-based material used to mimic the look of real leather. It is available in a variety of colors and patterns and is often used for accessories rather than apparel.

INGREDIENTS
- ☐ Standard heat transfer vinyl
- ☐ Base material, such as faux leather tote bag
- ☐ Cover sheet

EQUIPMENT
- ☐ Microfiber cloth
- ☐ Weeding tool
- ☐ Flat heat source such as a heat press
- ☐ (Optional) Pillow or foam to place inside bag

PREPARATION

Start with a new clean faux leather item, such as a tote bag, for best results. If item has any dust or debris, simply wipe off with a microfiber cloth.

Pre-heat your flat heat press to the temperature shown in chart below.

Place the vinyl with the carrier sheet side facing down on a machine mat and then use your cutting machine to **cut your desired pattern out of the vinyl. Weed as necessary** to remove any excess vinyl from the design.

Place the faux leather on top of the pressing pad.

Optionally, place a pressing pillow or foam insert inside the tote bag.

Place a cover sheet over the faux leather and **pre-heat for 5 seconds.**

Place the vinyl on the faux leather with the carrier sheet facing up.

Re-apply the cover sheet to the top of the vinyl carrier sheet.

Press according to the chart below.

Once you have applied the appropriate amount of heat and pressure, you can **slowly peel away your carrier sheet once cool to the touch.** If your vinyl peels away from the faux leather, carefully replace carrier sheet and apply a little more heat and pressure.

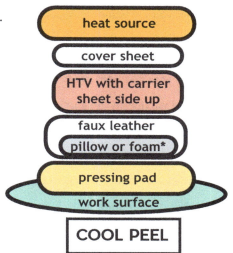

optional

COOK TIMES

Here are typical times you can use as a starting point. Always check the manufacturer's instructions for time and temperature, when available.

your favorite settings

Traditional Heat Press	AutoPress	EasyPress	Mini Press	
280°F / 138°C	280°F / 138°C	280°F / 138°C	Low	
10-15 seconds	15 seconds	30 seconds	30 seconds	
30 psi (Light pressure)	Auto pressure	Firm pressure	Firm pressure	

TIPS & TRICKS

- ✓ Remember to mirror your design if it contains words or phrases.
- ✗ Do not wash your item for at least 24 hours after applying the HTV. If you wash a garment, turn it inside out first.
- ✓ Check out the faux leather layered tote bag tutorial here jennifermaker.com/layer-iron-on-vinyl-cricut-tote-bag

STANDARD HTV

WOOD

Door sign, crate, cutting board, doorknob hanger, sign, yard sign, charcuterie board

Wood comes in a variety of finishes and can be painted or stained. Wood can be used both as flat panels and in the construction of 3D objects, such as crates.

INGREDIENTS
- ☐ Standard heat transfer vinyl
- ☐ Base material, such as unfinished wood round
- ☐ Cover sheet
- ☐ (Optional) Sandpaper

EQUIPMENT
- ☐ Microfiber cloth
- ☐ Weeding tool
- ☐ Scraper
- ☐ Flat heat source such as a heat press
- ☐ (Optional) Heat resistant tape

PREPARATION

Start with a new wood item, such as a wood sign, for the best results.

Start by prepping your wood. Optionally, sand the surface to remove any wood splinters and wipe with a cloth to remove any dust and debris.

Pre-heat your flat heat press to the temperature shown in chart below.

Place the vinyl with the carrier sheet side facing down on a machine mat and then use your cutting machine to **cut your desired pattern out of the vinyl. Weed as necessary** to remove any excess vinyl from the design.

Place your wood on the pressing pad and pre-press for 5 seconds.

Place the vinyl on the wood with the carrier sheet facing up.

Cover the carrier sheet with a cover sheet.

Press according to the chart below.

When the wood and vinyl are cool, gently peel away the carrier sheet.

If some parts of the vinyl start lifting off, replace the liner, heat the area for a few seconds, and use your scraper to press the hot vinyl into the wood. Then peel away the carrier sheet.

Stack (top to bottom): heat source / cover sheet / HTV with carrier sheet side up / wood / pressing pad / work surface

COOL PEEL

COOK TIMES
Here are typical times you can use as a starting point. Always check the manufacturer's instructions for time and temperature, when available.

your favorite settings

Traditional Heat Press	AutoPress	EasyPress	Mini Press	
305°F / 152°C	300°F / 149°C	300°F / 149°C	Medium	
15 seconds	40 seconds	40 seconds	40 seconds	
40 psi (Medium pressure)	Auto pressure	Firm pressure	Firm pressure	

TIPS & TRICKS
- ✓ Remember to mirror your design if it contains words or phrases.
- ✗ Do not wash your item for at least 24 hours after applying the HTV.
- ✓ Check out the tutorial on wood signs here jennifermaker.com/HTV-on-wood-signs
- ✓ It's normal to see a thin "halo" of adhesive around the edges of pressed vinyl on wood, but that it's important to minimize this halo by avoiding squishing out too much adhesive.

STANDARD HTV

CORK
Corkboard, coaster, serving tray, trivet, yoga block

Cork is a natural material that is lightweight and water-resistant. It can be flexible or made to be stiff and is usually used in home decor and accessories.

INGREDIENTS
☐ Standard heat transfer vinyl
☐ Base material, such as corkboard
☐ Cover sheet

EQUIPMENT
☐ Microfiber cloth
☐ Weeding tool
☐ Flat heat source such as a heat press
☐ (Optional) Ruler for placement help

PREPARATION

Start with a new cork item, such as a corkboard. Use a microfiber cloth to remove any dust or debris.

Pre-heat your flat heat press to the temperature shown in chart below.

Place the vinyl with the carrier sheet side facing down on a machine mat and then use your cutting machine to **cut your desired pattern out of the vinyl. Weed as necessary** to remove any excess vinyl from the design.

Place your cork on top of your pressing pad.

Pre-press the board for 5 seconds to eliminate any moisture.

Place the vinyl on the cork with the carrier sheet facing up.

Cover the carrier sheet with a cover sheet to help protect the vinyl and the cork.

Press according to the chart below.

Once you have applied the appropriate amount of heat and pressure, you can **slowly peel away your carrier sheet after it cools.** If your vinyl peels away from the cork, carefully replace carrier sheet and apply a little more heat and pressure.

Stack (top to bottom): heat source, cover sheet, HTV with carrier sheet side up, cork, pressing pad, work surface. **COOL PEEL**

COOK TIMES
Here are typical times you can use as a starting point. Always check the manufacturer's instructions for time and temperature, when available.

your favorite settings

Traditional Heat Press	AutoPress	EasyPress	Mini Press	
315°F / 157°C	315°F / 157°C	315°F / 157°C	Medium	
30 seconds	15 seconds	15 seconds	25 seconds	
50 psi (Firm pressure)	Auto pressure	Firm pressure	Firm pressure	

TIPS & TRICKS
✓ Remember to mirror your design if it contains words or phrases.
✓ To clean, use a microfiber cloth.
✓ Check out a tutorial on customized cork coasters here jennifermaker.com/custom-cork-coasters/
✓ To prevent cork for curling after pressing place a heavy book on top while it cools.

STANDARD HTV

NEOPRENE

Drink sleeve, chapstick holder, coaster, flip flops, kneeling pad, laptop sleeve, lunch bag, mousepad, sanitizer bottle holder

Neoprene is a synthetic rubber material that is often used for insulation of heated or cooled items. HTV can easily be applied; however, be cautious as this material can scorch or distort when too much heat is applied.

INGREDIENTS
☐ Standard heat transfer vinyl
☐ Base material, such as neoprene drink sleeve
☐ Cover sheets

EQUIPMENT
☐ Lint roller
☐ Weeding tool
☐ Flat heat source such as a heat press
☐ (Optional) Ruler for placement help
☐ (Optional) Heat-resistant tape

PREPARATION

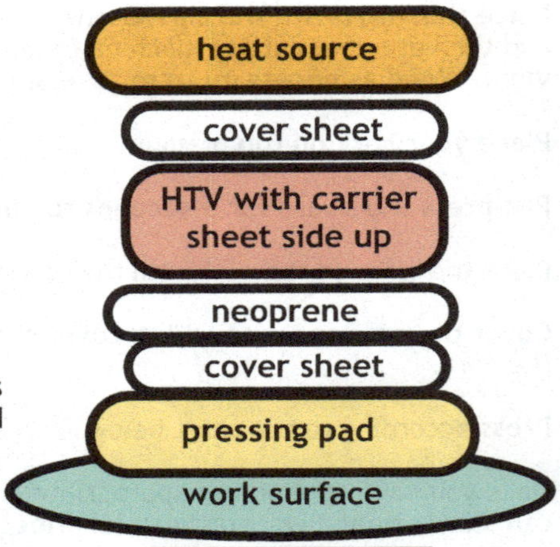

Start with a new neoprene item, such as a neoprene drink sleeve.

Use a **lint roller** if necessary to remove dust and debris.

Pre-heat your flat heat press to the temperature shown in chart below.

Place the vinyl with the carrier sheet side facing down on a machine mat and then use your cutting machine to **cut your desired pattern out of the vinyl. Weed as necessary** to remove any excess vinyl from the design.

Place a cover sheet on top of your pressing pad.

Place the neoprene on top of the cover sheet and flatten it with the seams at the sides. Place another piece of cover sheet on top of the neoprene and then **pre-heat for 5 seconds. Remove** the top cover sheet.

Place the vinyl on the neoprene with the carrier sheet facing up.

Using heat-resistant tape, **secure the vinyl to the neoprene.**

Place the **cover sheet on top of the vinyl carrier sheet.**

Press according to the chart below.

Once the drink sleeve has cooled, **slowly remove the carrier sheet**. If your vinyl peels away from the neoprene, carefully replace carrier sheet and apply a little more heat and pressure.

Layers (top to bottom):
- heat source
- cover sheet
- HTV with carrier sheet side up
- neoprene
- cover sheet
- pressing pad
- work surface

COOL PEEL

COOK TIMES

Here are typical times you can use as a starting point. Always check the manufacturer's instructions for time and temperature, when available.

your favorite settings

Traditional Heat Press	AutoPress	EasyPress	Mini Press	
280°F / 138°C	280°F / 138°C	280°F / 138°C	Medium	
20 seconds	15 seconds	20 seconds	20 seconds	
40 psi (Medium pressure)	Auto pressure	Firm pressure	Firm pressure	

TIPS & TRICKS
✓ Remember to mirror your design if it contains words or phrases.
✗ Do not wash your item for at least 24 hours after applying the HTV. If possible, turn item inside out before washing.

STANDARD HTV

CERAMIC
Coaster, tile, trivet

Ceramic is a product formed by clay that has been hardened by high heat. There are many types of ceramic items, such as mugs; however, this recipe is for a flat ceramic item.

INGREDIENTS
- ☐ Standard heat transfer vinyl
- ☐ Base material, such as ceramic coaster
- ☐ (Optional) Cover sheet

EQUIPMENT
- ☐ Rubbing alcohol
- ☐ Microfiber cloth
- ☐ Weeding tool
- ☐ Flat heat source such as a heat press
- ☐ (Optional) Heat-resistant tape

PREPARATION

Start with a new flat ceramic item, such as a coaster, for the best results.

Pre-heat your heat press to the temperatures shown in the chart below.

Use the rubbing alcohol and microfiber cloth to gently clean the surface of the ceramic. Let dry completely.

Place the vinyl with the carrier sheet side facing down on a machine mat and then use your cutting machine to **cut your desired pattern out of the vinyl. Weed as necessary** to remove any excess vinyl from the design.

Place the ceramic on top of your pressing pad.

Place the vinyl on the ceramic with the carrier sheet facing up.

Optionally, cover the ceramic and vinyl with a cover sheet.

Press according to the chart below.

Let cool, then slowly **peel the carrier sheet away.**

If the vinyl peels away from the ceramic, **carefully replace carrier sheet and apply a little more heat and pressure.**

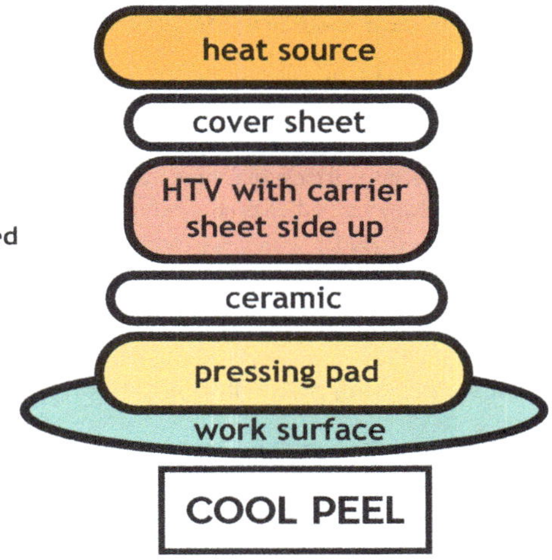

Stack (top to bottom):
- heat source
- cover sheet
- HTV with carrier sheet side up
- ceramic
- pressing pad
- work surface

COOL PEEL

COOK TIMES
Here are typical times you can use as a starting point. Always check the manufacturer's instructions for time and temperature, when available.

your favorite settings

Traditional Heat Press	AutoPress	EasyPress	Mini Press	
320°F / 160°C	300°F / 149°C	300°F / 149°C	High	
25 seconds	30 seconds	30 seconds	30 seconds	
40 psi (Medium pressure)	Auto pressure	Medium pressure	Medium pressure	

TIPS & TRICKS
- ✓ Remember to mirror your design if it contains words or phrases.
- ✓ Wash with soap and water, or just a damp cloth.

STANDARD HTV

POLYPROPYLENE
Bag, sportswear, furniture upholstery

Polypropylene is a synthetic non-woven fabric that is lightweight and is often used for sportswear, bags, and furniture upholstery. It has a low melting point, so it cannot be exposed to high heat for a long time.

INGREDIENTS
☐ Standard heat transfer vinyl
☐ Base material, such as polypropylene bag
☐ Cover sheet

EQUIPMENT
☐ Lint roller
☐ Weeding tool
☐ Flat heat source such as a heat press
☐ Pressing pillow/foam

PREPARATION

Start with a new polypropylene item, such as a bag, for the best results.

Pre-heat your heat press to the temperatures shown in the chart below.

Use a lint roller to remove and dust and debris from the polpropylene material.

Place the vinyl with the carrier sheet side facing down on a machine mat and then use your cutting machine to **cut your desired pattern out of the vinyl. Weed as necessary** to remove any excess vinyl from the design.

Place the **polypropylene material on top** of your pressing pad.

Place the vinyl on the polypropylene material with the **carrier sheet facing up.**

Place a pressing pillow inside the polypropylene material, if possible.

Cover the polypropylene material and vinyl with **a cover sheet.**

Press according to the chart below.

Let cool, then slowly **peel the carrier sheet away.**

If the vinyl peels away from the polypropylene, **carefully replace carrier sheet and apply a little more heat and pressure for 5 seconds at a time.**

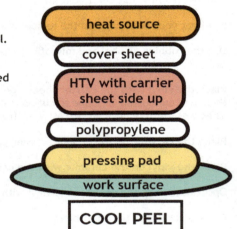

COOK TIMES
Here are typical times you can use as a starting point. Always check the manufacturer's instructions for time and temperature, when available.

your favorite settings

Traditional Heat Press	AutoPress	EasyPress	Mini Press	
270°F / 132°C	270°F / 132°C	270°F / 132°C	Medium	
5 seconds	5 seconds	5 seconds	5 seconds	
40 psi (Medium pressure)	Auto pressure	Medium pressure	Medium pressure	

TIPS & TRICKS
✓ Remember to mirror your design if it contains words or phrases.
✓ Be sure to use a cover sheet when pressing polypropylene, just in case it does melt, to avoid getting anything on your platen.
✓ Be sure to do a test press in an inconspicuous spot on on your polypropylene just in case it wants to melt even at these recommended settings.

CHAPTER 2
FLEX/STRETCH HTV

FLEX/STRETCH HTV

ATHLETIC MESH/JERSEY
Athletic jersey, athletic shirt, athletic skirt, athletic shorts

Athletic mesh fabric is durable and is commonly used for sports jerseys. The material comes in both micro-mesh and standard mesh sizes, providing a little bit of diversity in aesthetics.

INGREDIENTS
- ☐ Flex/Stretch heat transfer vinyl
- ☐ Base material, such as athletic mesh jersey
- ☐ Cover sheet

EQUIPMENT
- ☐ Lint roller
- ☐ Weeding tool
- ☐ Flat heat source such as a heat press
- ☐ (Optional) T-shirt ruler for placement help
- ☐ (Optional) Pillow or foam insert

PREPARATION

Start with a new athletic mesh item, such as a jersey, for the best results. No need to pre-wash, but if you do, avoid fabric softener.

Pre-heat your flat heat press to the temperature shown in chart below.

Place the vinyl with the carrier sheet side facing down on a machine mat and then use your cutting machine to **cut your desired pattern out of the vinyl. Weed as necessary** to remove any excess vinyl from the design.

Use a lint roller to remove any lint or fibers from the athletic mesh.

Fold the athletic mesh in half lengthwise so both sides match up, cover with a cover sheet, then **press for 10 seconds** — this both pre-heats the shirt to remove moisture and gives you a straight vertical crease for alignment.

Unfold the athletic mesh and lay it flat. Optionally, slide a pressing pillow or foam insert inside the athletic mesh to provide additional support.

Place the vinyl on the athletic mesh with the carrier sheet facing up.

Cover the carrier sheet and vinyl with a cover sheet to help avoid overheating the vinyl or melting the athletic mesh.

Press according to the chart below.

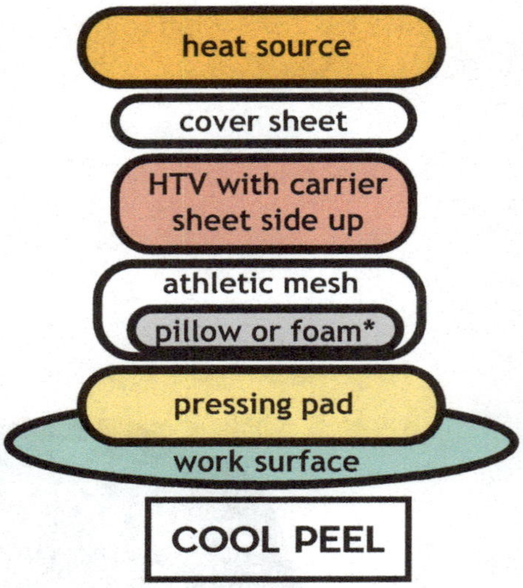

Let cool, then slowly peel away the carrier sheet. If the vinyl peels away from the athletic mesh, carefully replace the carrier sheet and apply a little more heat and pressure for a short amount of time.

Stack (top to bottom):
- heat source
- cover sheet
- HTV with carrier sheet side up
- athletic mesh
- pillow or foam*
- pressing pad
- work surface

COOL PEEL

optional

COOK TIMES
Here are typical times you can use as a starting point. Always check the manufacturer's instructions for time and temperature, when available.

Traditional Heat Press	AutoPress	EasyPress	Mini Press	your favorite settings
305°F / 152°C	305°F / 152°C	305°F / 152°C	Low	
25 seconds	25 seconds	30 seconds	40 seconds	
50 psi (Firm pressure)	Auto pressure	Firm pressure	Firm pressure	

TIPS & TRICKS
- ✗ Do not wash your item for at least 24 hours after applying the HTV. If you wash a garment, turn it inside out first.
- ✓ Do not use bleach. Wash on gentle cycle and tumble dry low or hang to dry.

FLEX/STRETCH HTV

STRETCH POLYESTER

Long-sleeved shirt, backpack, blanket, dress, hoodie, infant bodysuit, lounge pants, pajamas, pillowcase, plushie, polo shirt, shorts, tank top, t-shirt

Polyester is a blend of synthetic materials and is one of the most commonly used materials for textiles. Heat transfer vinyl is easily applied with low heat and medium to firm pressure.

INGREDIENTS
☐ Flex/Stretch heat transfer vinyl
☐ Base material, such as long-sleeved shirt
☐ Cover sheet

EQUIPMENT
☐ Lint roller
☐ Weeding tool
☐ Flat heat source such as a heat press
☐ (Optional) T-shirt ruler for placement help
☐ (Optional) Pillow or foam insert

PREPARATION

Start with a new stretch polyester item, such as a long-sleeved shirt, for the best results. No need to pre-wash, but if you do, avoid fabric softener.

Pre-heat your flat heat press to the temperature shown in chart below.

Place the vinyl with the carrier sheet side facing down on a machine mat and then use your cutting machine to **cut your desired pattern out of the vinyl. Weed as necessary** to remove any excess vinyl from the design.

Use a lint roller to remove any dust or fibers from the stretch polyester.

If you're pressing a shirt, **fold the shirt in half lengthwise** so both sides match up, then **press for 5 seconds** — this both pre-heats the shirt to remove moisture and gives you a straight vertical crease for alignment.

Unfold the shirt and lay it flat. Optionally, slide a pressing pillow or foam insert inside the shirt to provide additional support. **Do not stretch the fabric.**

Place the vinyl on the stretch polyester with the carrier sheet facing up.

Cover the carrier sheet and vinyl with a cover sheet to help avoid overheating the vinyl.

Press according to the chart below.

Let cool, then slowly peel away the carrier sheet.

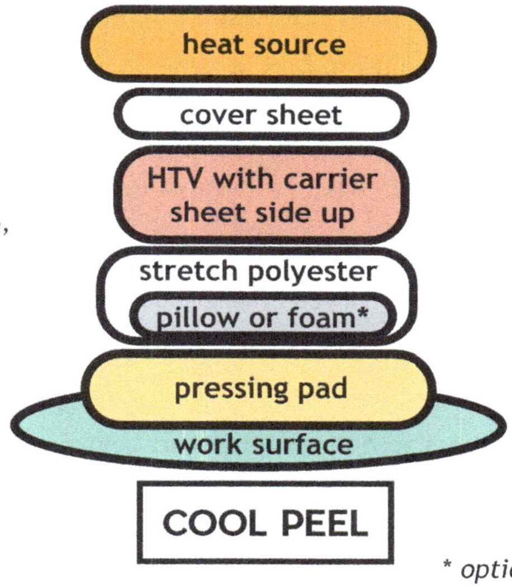

Layers (bottom to top): work surface, pressing pad, pillow or foam*, stretch polyester, HTV with carrier sheet side up, cover sheet, heat source.

COOL PEEL

optional

COOK TIMES
Here are typical times you can use as a starting point. Always check the manufacturer's instructions for time and temperature, when available.

Traditional Heat Press	AutoPress	EasyPress	Mini Press	your favorite settings
305°F / 152°C	305°F / 152°C	305°F / 152°C	Medium	
30 seconds	30 seconds	30 seconds	30 seconds	
50 psi (Firm pressure)	Auto pressure	Firm pressure	Firm pressure	

TIPS & TRICKS
✓ Check out a tutorial at jennifermaker.com/cricut-vinyl-projects

FLEX/STRETCH HTV

SPANDEX
Bike shorts, dress, headband, leggings, leotard, tank top, t-shirt

Spandex is a synthetic fabric that is very stretchy without losing its shape. It is ideal for athletic apparel.

INGREDIENTS
- ☐ Flex/Stretch heat transfer vinyl
- ☐ Base material, such as bike shorts
- ☐ Cover sheet

EQUIPMENT
- ☐ Lint roller
- ☐ Weeding tool
- ☐ Flat heat source such as a heat press
- ☐ (Optional) T-shirt ruler for placement help
- ☐ (Optional) Pillow or foam insert

PREPARATION

Start with a new spandex item, such as a pair of bike shorts, for the best results. No need to pre-wash, but if you do, avoid fabric softener.

Pre-heat your flat heat press to the temperature shown in chart below.

Place the vinyl with the carrier sheet side facing down on a machine mat and then use your cutting machine to **cut your desired pattern out of the vinyl. Weed as necessary** to remove any excess vinyl from the design.

Use a lint roller to remove any dust or fibers from the spandex.

Cover the spandex with a cover sheet and pre-heat for 10 seconds.

For bike shorts, optionally slide small pressing pillows or foam inserts inside the legs of the bike shorts to provide additional support. **Do not stretch the fabric.**

Place the vinyl on the spandex with the carrier sheet facing up.

Cover the carrier sheet and vinyl with a cover sheet to help avoid overheating the vinyl.

Press according to the chart below.

Let cool, then slowly peel away the carrier sheet. If the vinyl peels away from the spandex, carefully replace the carrier sheet and apply a little more heat and pressure for a short amount of time.

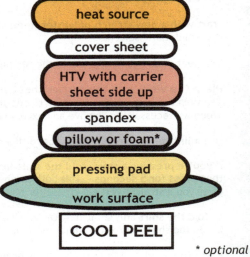

COOK TIMES
Here are typical times you can use as a starting point. Always check the manufacturer's instructions for time and temperature, when available.

your favorite settings

Traditional Heat Press	AutoPress	EasyPress	Mini Press	
280°F / 138°C	280°F / 138°C	280°F / 138°C	Low	
15 seconds	15 seconds	15 seconds	20 seconds	
40 psi (Medium pressure)	Auto pressure	Medium pressure	Medium pressure	

TIPS & TRICKS
- ✓ Remember to mirror your design if it contains words or phrases.
- ✗ Make sure your pillow or foam insert does not stretch the fabric. If it does, the vinyl will wrinkle.
- ✗ Do not wash your item for at least 24 hours after applying the HTV. If you wash a garment, turn it inside out first.

FLEX/STRETCH HTV

NYLON

Windbreaker, activewear, backpack, drawstring bag, poncho, puff vest, swimwear, tech accessory bag, umbrella

Nylon is a synthetic fabric with a variety of uses. It can melt or burn, so extra care is needed when applying heat transfer vinyl.

INGREDIENTS
☐ Flex/Stretch heat transfer vinyl
☐ Base material, such as windbreaker
☐ Cover sheet

EQUIPMENT
☐ Lint roller
☐ Weeding tool
☐ Flat heat source such as a heat press
☐ (Optional) T-shirt ruler for placement help
☐ (Optional) Pillow or foam insert

PREPARATION

Start with a new nylon item, such as a windbreaker, for the best results. No need to pre-wash, but if you do, avoid fabric softener.

Pre-heat your flat heat press to the temperature shown in chart below.

Place the vinyl with the carrier sheet side facing down on a machine mat and then use your cutting machine to **cut your desired pattern out of the vinyl. Weed as necessary** to remove any excess vinyl from the design.

Use a lint roller to remove any dust or fibers from the nylon.

Cover the nylon with a cover sheet and pre-press for 5 seconds, taking care to avoid any plastic zippers or buttons. Remove the cover sheet.

Lay the nylon flat. Optionally, slide a pressing pillow or foam insert inside to provide additional support.

Place the vinyl on the nylon with the carrier sheet facing up.

Cover the carrier sheet and vinyl with a cover sheet to help avoid overheating the vinyl or melting the nylon.

Press according to the chart below.

Let cool, then slowly peel away the carrier sheet. If the vinyl peels away from the nylon, carefully replace the carrier sheet and apply a little more heat and pressure for a short amount of time.

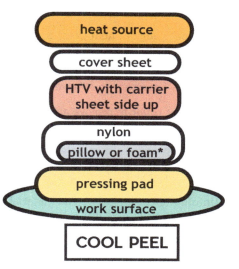

COOL PEEL

* optional

COOK TIMES
Here are typical times you can use as a starting point. Always check the manufacturer's instructions for time and temperature, when available.

your favorite settings

Traditional Heat Press	AutoPress	EasyPress	Mini Press	
305°F / 152°C	305°F / 152°C	305°F / 152°C	Low	
20 seconds	15 seconds	30 seconds	30 sec then flip +15 sec	
50 psi (Firm pressure)	Auto pressure	Firm pressure	Firm pressure	

TIPS & TRICKS
✓ In addition to the body of the windbreaker, vinyl can be applied to the sleeves and hood as well.
✗ Do not wash your item for at least 24 hours after applying the HTV. If you wash a garment, turn it inside out first.

FLEX/STRETCH HTV

COTTON/POLY BLEND

Tank top, blanket, burp cloth, dress, hoodie, infant bodysuit, long-sleeved shirt, lounge pants, pajamas, pillowcase, plushie, polo shirt, shorts, sweatshirt, t-shirt

Cotton blends, often found as 50/50 cotton/polyester, of any color are a popular base material for flex/stretch heat transfer vinyl. The vinyl can be applied anywhere on the shirt.

INGREDIENTS
- ☐ Flex/Stretch heat transfer vinyl
- ☐ Base material, such as cotton/poly tank top
- ☐ Cover sheet

EQUIPMENT
- ☐ Lint roller
- ☐ Weeding tool
- ☐ Flat heat source such as a heat press
- ☐ (Optional) T-shirt ruler for placement help
- ☐ (Optional) Pillow or foam insert

PREPARATION

Start with a new cotton/polyester blend item, such as a tank top, for the best results. No need to pre-wash, but if you do, avoid fabric softener.

Pre-heat your flat heat press to the temperature shown in chart below.

Place the vinyl with the carrier sheet side facing down on a machine mat and then use your cutting machine to **cut your desired pattern out of the vinyl. Weed as necessary** to remove any excess vinyl from the design.

Use a lint roller to remove any dust or fibers from the cotton/poly blend material.

If you're pressing a shirt, fold the shirt in half lengthwise so both sides match up, then **press for 5 seconds** — this both pre-heats the shirt to remove moisture and gives you a straight vertical crease for alignment.

Unfold the cotton/poly blend material **and lay it flat.** Optionally, slide a pressing pillow or foam insert inside the tank top to provide additional support.

Place the vinyl on the cotton/poly blend material **with the carrier sheet facing up.**

Cover the carrier sheet and vinyl with a cover sheet in order to avoid overheating the vinyl.

Press according to the chart below.

Let cool, then slowly peel away the carrier sheet.

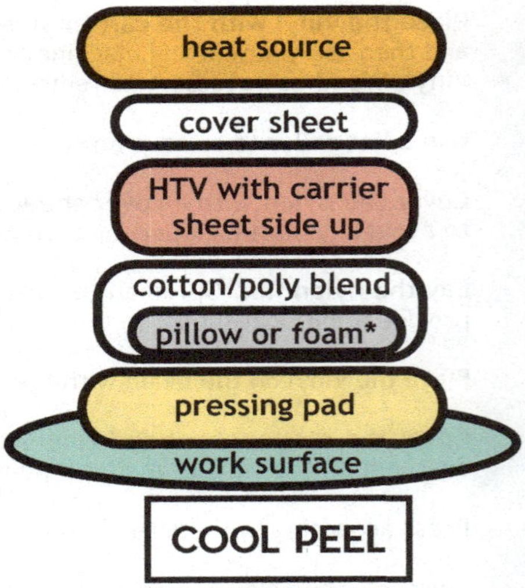

Stack (top to bottom):
- heat source
- cover sheet
- HTV with carrier sheet side up
- cotton/poly blend
- pillow or foam*
- pressing pad
- work surface

COOL PEEL

optional

COOK TIMES

Here are typical times you can use as a starting point. Always check the manufacturer's instructions for time and temperature, when available.

your favorite settings

Traditional Heat Press	AutoPress	EasyPress	Mini Press	
345°F /174°C	345°F /174°C	345°F /174°C	Medium	
45 seconds	45 seconds	50 seconds	55 seconds	
40 psi (Medium pressure)	Auto pressure	Medium pressure	Medium pressure	

TIPS & TRICKS
- ✓ Remember to mirror your design if it contains words or phrases.
- ✓ If your tank top is ribbed, do not allow a pressing pillow/foam to stretch it out before applying vinyl.

POLY/NYLON BLEND

Dress, backpack, door mat, infant bodysuit, long-sleeved shirt, pants, polo shirt, shorts, tank top, t-shirt, tote bag

Polyester/nylon blend fabric is made of synthetic material. It is more durable than polyester alone and softer than nylon alone.

INGREDIENTS

- ☐ Flex/Stretch heat transfer vinyl
- ☐ Base material, such as poly/nylon dress
- ☐ Cover sheet

EQUIPMENT

- ☐ Lint roller
- ☐ Weeding tool
- ☐ Flat heat source such as a heat press
- ☐ (Optional) T-shirt ruler for placement help
- ☐ (Optional) Pillow or foam

PREPARATION

Start with a new polyester/nylon blend item, such as a dress, for the best results. No need to pre-wash, but if you do, avoid fabric softener.

Pre-heat your flat heat press to the temperature shown in chart below.

Place the vinyl with the carrier sheet side facing down on a machine mat and then use your cutting machine to **cut your desired pattern out of the vinyl**. **Weed as necessary** to remove any excess vinyl from the design.

Use a lint roller to remove any dust or fibers from the poly/nylon blend material.

Cover the poly/nylon blend material **with a cover sheet and pre-press for 5 seconds.**

Unfold the poly/nylon blend material **and lay it flat.** Optionally, slide a pressing pillow or foam insert inside the part of the poly/nylon blend material you are going to apply vinyl to in order to provide additional support.

Place the vinyl on the poly/nylon blend material **with the carrier sheet facing up.**

Cover the carrier sheet and vinyl with a cover sheet to help avoid overheating the vinyl.

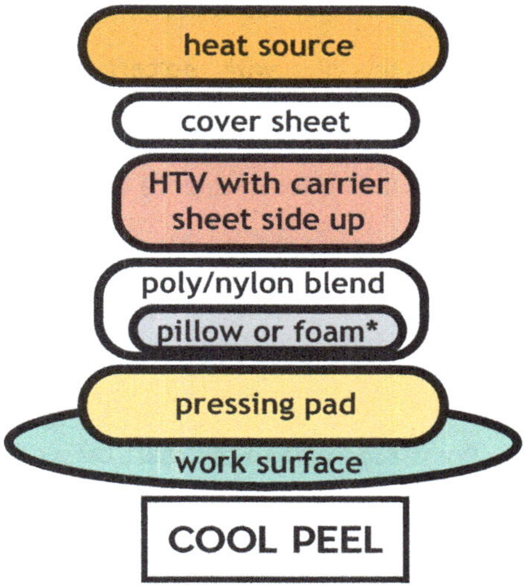
heat source
cover sheet
HTV with carrier sheet side up
poly/nylon blend
pillow or foam*
pressing pad
work surface
COOL PEEL

** optional*

Press according to the chart below.

Let cool, then slowly peel away the carrier sheet. If the vinyl peels away from the poly/nylon blend material, carefully replace the carrier sheet and apply a little more heat and pressure for a short amount of time.

COOK TIMES

Here are typical times you can use as a starting point. Always check the manufacturer's instructions for time and temperature, when available.

your favorite settings

Traditional Heat Press	AutoPress	EasyPress	Mini Press	
305°F / 152°C	305°F / 152°C	305°F / 152°C	Medium	
25 seconds	25 seconds	30 seconds	40 seconds	
50 psi (Firm pressure)	Auto pressure	Firm pressure	Firm pressure	

TIPS & TRICKS

- ✓ Remember to mirror your design if it contains words or phrases.
- ✓ If your dress has pleats, spread them out flat before applying vinyl to that area.

FLEX/STRETCH HTV

NEOPRENE

Car coaster, chapstick holder, drink sleeve, flip flops, kneeling pad, laptop sleeve, lunch bag, mousepad, sanitizer bottle holder

Neoprene is a synthetic rubber material that is often used for insulation of heated or cooled items.

INGREDIENTS
☐ Flex/Stretch heat transfer vinyl
☐ Base material, such as neoprene car coaster(s)
☐ Cover sheets

EQUIPMENT
☐ Lint roller
☐ Weeding tool
☐ Flat heat source such as a heat press
☐ (Optional) Ruler for placement help

PREPARATION

Start with a new neoprene item, such as coasters, for the best results.

Pre-heat your flat heat press to the temperature shown in chart below.

Place the vinyl with the carrier sheet side facing down on a machine mat and then use your cutting machine to **cut your desired pattern out of the vinyl. Weed as necessary** to remove any excess vinyl from the design.

Use a lint roller to remove any dust or fibers from the neoprene.

Place a cover sheet on the pressing pad, then place the neoprene on top.

Place the vinyl on the neoprene with the carrier sheet facing up.

Cover the carrier sheet and vinyl with a cover sheet to help avoid overheating the vinyl or the material.

Press according to the chart below.

Let cool, then slowly peel away the carrier sheet. If the vinyl peels away from the neoprene, carefully replace the carrier sheet and apply a little more heat and pressure for a short amount of time.

Stack order (top to bottom):
- heat source
- cover sheet
- HTV with carrier sheet side up
- neoprene
- pressing pad
- work surface

COOL PEEL

COOK TIMES
Here are typical times you can use as a starting point. Always check the manufacturer's instructions for time and temperature, when available.

your favorite settings

Traditional Heat Press	AutoPress	EasyPress	Mini Press	
280°F / 138°C	280°F / 138°C	280°F / 138°C	Medium	
20 seconds	20 seconds	20 seconds	20 seconds	
50 psi (Firm pressure)	Auto pressure	Firm pressure	Firm pressure	

TIPS & TRICKS
✓ Remember to mirror your design if it contains words or phrases.
✓ If using a traditional heat press, AutoPress, or large EasyPress, you can press multiple coasters at one time.
✗ Wait 24 hours before using coasters so that the sweat from drinks does not affect the vinyl adhesive.
✓ These coasters work well in any setting, not just in car cup holders.
✗ Do not wash your item for at least 24 hours after applying the HTV. If possible, turn item inside out before washing.

FLEX/STRETCH HTV

SISER EASYWEED STRETCH HTV

Athletic shirts, athletic shorts, athletic skirts, performance wear, leggings, leotards, jerseys

Siser Stretch is a flexible, stretchy heat transfer vinyl that can be used on cotton, polyester, cotton/polyester blends, leather, faux leather, and spandex.

INGREDIENTS
☐ Siser EasyWeed Stretch heat transfer vinyl
☐ Base material, such as stretchy T-shirt
☐ Cover sheet

EQUIPMENT
☐ Lint roller
☐ Weeding tool
☐ Flat heat source such as a heat press
☐ (Optional) Ruler for placement help

PREPARATION

Start with a new garment, such as a T-shirt, for the best results. No need to pre-wash, but if you do, avoid fabric softener.

Pre-heat your flat heat press to the temperature shown in chart below.

Place the vinyl with the carrier sheet side facing down on a machine mat and then use your cutting machine to **cut your desired pattern out of the vinyl. Weed as necessary** to remove any excess vinyl from the design.

Use a lint roller to remove any dust or fibers from the garment.

If you're pressing a shirt, fold the shirt in half lengthwise so both sides match up, then **press for 5 seconds** — this both pre-heats the shirt to remove moisture and gives you a straight vertical crease for alignment.

Unfold the garment and lay it flat.

Place the vinyl on the garment with the carrier sheet facing up.

Cover the carrier sheet and vinyl with a cover sheet to help avoid overheating the vinyl.

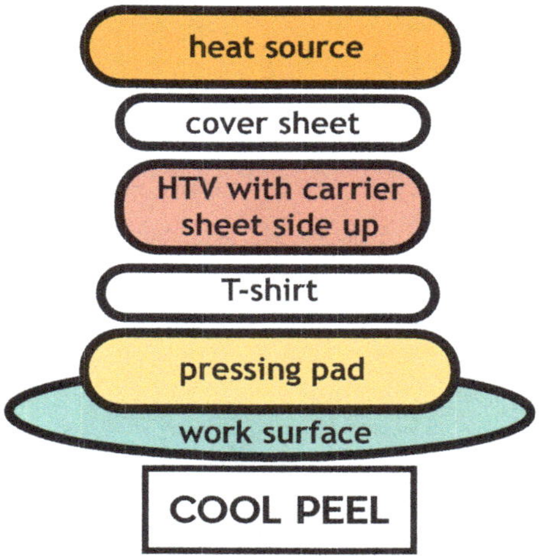

Press according to the chart below.

Let cool completely, then slowly peel away the carrier sheet. If the vinyl peels away from the garment, carefully replace the carrier sheet and apply a little more heat and pressure for a short amount of time.

Layer stack (top to bottom): heat source / cover sheet / HTV with carrier sheet side up / T-shirt / pressing pad / work surface — **COOL PEEL**

COOK TIMES
Here are typical times you can use as a starting point. Always check the manufacturer's instructions for time and temperature, when available.

your favorite settings

Traditional Heat Press	AutoPress	EasyPress	Mini Press	
305°F / 152°C	320°F / 160°C	335°F / 168°C	Medium	
20 seconds	20 seconds	20 seconds	20 seconds	
50 psi (Firm Pressure)	Firm pressure	Firm pressure	Firm pressure	

TIPS & TRICKS
✓ If using a home iron, do not slide the iron around it can cause the vinyl to wrinkle.

CHAPTER 3
MESH HTV

MESH HTV

BURLAP

Garden flag, bag, banner, bunting, pillowcase, table runner, wine bag, wreath

Burlap is a material made of plant fibers. Natural burlap comes in shades of brown, but it can be dyed any color. Burlap fabric is textured and can be tightly or loosely woven.

INGREDIENTS
- ☐ Mesh heat transfer vinyl
- ☐ Base material, such as burlap garden flag
- ☐ Cover sheet

EQUIPMENT
- ☐ Lint roller
- ☐ Weeding tool
- ☐ Flat heat source such as a heat press
- ☐ (Optional) Ruler for placement help

PREPARATION

Start with a new burlap item, such as a garden flag, for the best results.

Pre-heat your flat heat press to the temperature shown in chart below.

Place the vinyl with the carrier sheet side facing down on a machine mat and then use your cutting machine to **cut your desired pattern out of the vinyl. Weed as necessary** to remove any excess vinyl from the design.

Use the lint roller to clean any dust, debris, or loose fibers on the burlap.

Pre-press your burlap for 5 seconds to remove any wrinkles, then **fold your burlap in half and press for an additional 5 seconds** to create a crease in the center this will help align the vinyl.

Place the vinyl on the burlap with the carrier sheet facing up.

Cover the carrier sheet and vinyl with a cover sheet to help avoid overheating the vinyl.

Press according to the chart below.

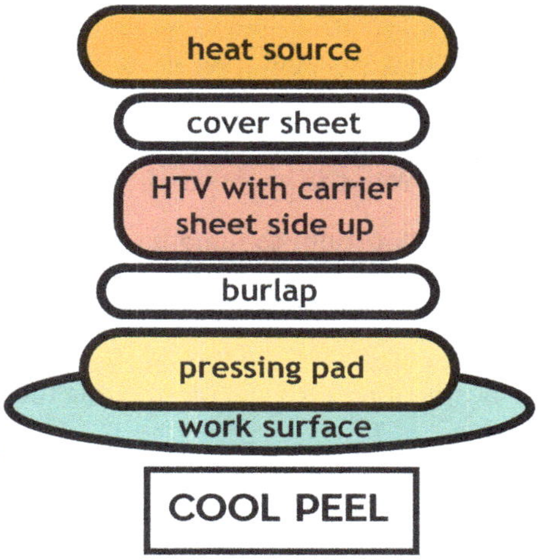

Let cool slightly, then **slowly peel away the carrier sheet once cool to the touch.** If the vinyl peels away from the burlap, carefully replace the carrier sheet and apply a little more heat and pressure for a short amount of time.

Repeat steps to apply vinyl to the other side, if desired.

Stack order (bottom to top): work surface, pressing pad, burlap, HTV with carrier sheet side up, cover sheet, heat source.

COOL PEEL

COOK TIMES

Here are typical times you can use as a starting point. Always check the manufacturer's instructions for time and temperature, when available.

your favorite settings

Traditional Heat Press	AutoPress	EasyPress	Mini Press	
305°F / 152°C	305°F / 152°C	305°F / 152°C	Medium	
45-60 seconds	20 seconds	30 seconds	30 sec then flip +15 sec	
50 psi (Firm pressure)	Auto pressure	Firm pressure	Firm pressure	

TIPS & TRICKS
- ✗ Do not wash your item for at least 24 hours after applying the HTV.
- ✓ Remember to mirror your design if it contains words or phrases.

MESH HTV

NYLON

Jogging shorts, activewear, backpack, drawstring bag, poncho, puff vest, swimwear, tech accessory bag, umbrella, windbreaker

Nylon is a synthetic fabric with a variety of uses. It can melt or burn, so extra care is needed when applying heat transfer vinyl.

INGREDIENTS
☐ Mesh heat transfer vinyl
☐ Base material, such as nylon jogging shorts
☐ Cover sheet

EQUIPMENT
☐ Lint roller
☐ Weeding tool
☐ Flat heat source such as a heat press

PREPARATION

Start with new nylon item, such as a pair of jogging shorts, for the best results. No need to pre-wash, but if you do, avoid fabric softener.

Pre-heat your flat heat press to the temperature shown in chart below.

Place the vinyl with the carrier sheet side facing down on a machine mat and then use your cutting machine to **cut your desired pattern out of the vinyl. Weed as necessary** to remove any excess vinyl from the design.

Use a lint roller to remove any dust or fibers from the nylon.

Place the vinyl on the nylon with the carrier sheet facing up.

Cover the carrier sheet and vinyl with a cover sheet to help avoid overheating the vinyl and melting the nylon base.

Press according to the chart below.

Let cool slightly, then **slowly peel away the carrier sheet once cool to the touch.** If the vinyl peels away from the nylon, carefully replace the carrier sheet and apply a little more heat and pressure for a short amount of time.

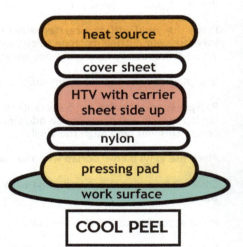

COOL PEEL

COOK TIMES
Here are typical times you can use as a starting point. Always check the manufacturer's instructions for time and temperature, when available.

your favorite settings

Traditional Heat Press	AutoPress	EasyPress	Mini Press	
280°F / 138°C	280°F / 138°C	280°F / 138°C	Low	
30 seconds	30 seconds	30 seconds	30 sec then flip +15 sec	
40 psi (Firm pressure)	Auto pressure	Firm pressure	Firm pressure	

TIPS & TRICKS
✗ Do not wash your item for at least 24 hours after applying the HTV. If you wash a garment, turn it inside out first.
✓ Remember to mirror your design if it contains words or phrases.

MESH HTV

CANVAS

Drawstring tote, art canvas, backdrop, cooler, flag, reverse art canvas, placemat, sail, shoes, tent

Make sure your canvas is made of polyester or cotton and does not have any plastic components, which can melt. Plain canvas is usually cream to tan, but can be dyed any color. Canvas fabric can be very smooth or more roughly textured.

INGREDIENTS
☐ Mesh heat transfer vinyl
☐ Base material, such as canvas drawstring tote bag
☐ Cover sheet

EQUIPMENT
☐ Lint roller
☐ Weeding tool
☐ Flat heat source such as a heat press
☐ (Optional) Pressing pillow or foam insert

PREPARATION

Start with a new canvas item, such as a blank canvas tote bag.

Pre-heat your flat heat press to the temperature shown in chart below.

Place the vinyl with the carrier sheet side facing down on a machine mat and then use your cutting machine to **cut your desired pattern out of the vinyl. Weed as necessary** to remove any excess vinyl from the design.

Place your canvas on top of the pressing pad. **Pre-press** for 5 seconds.

Optionally, place a pressing pillow or foam insert inside the canvas.

Place the vinyl on the canvas with the carrier sheet facing up. Cover the carrier sheet with a cover sheet to help avoid overheating or scorching the vinyl.

Press according to the chart below.

Once you have applied the appropriate amount of heat and pressure, allow the tote bag to cool before you **slowly peel away your carrier sheet**.

If your vinyl peels away from the canvas, carefully replace carrier sheet and apply a little more heat and pressure.

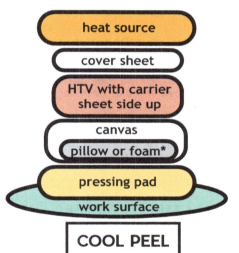

* optional

COOK TIMES
Here are typical times you can use as a starting point. Always check the manufacturer's instructions for time and temperature, when available.

your favorite settings

Traditional Heat Press	AutoPress	EasyPress	Mini Press	
340°F / 171°C	340°F / 171°C	340°F / 171°C	Medium	
25 seconds	20 seconds	30 seconds	25 seconds	
50 psi (Firm pressure)	Auto pressure	Firm pressure	Firm pressure	

TIPS & TRICKS
✗ Do not wash your item for at least 24 hours after applying the HTV.
✓ Remember to mirror your design if it contains words or phrases.

MESH HTV

COTTON

Burp cloth, blanket, denim, dress, hoodie, infant bodysuit, long-sleeved shirt, lounge pants, pajamas, pillowcase, plushie, polo shirt, shorts, sweatshirt, tank top, t-shirt

Items made from 100% cotton work well for heat transfer vinyl. The versatility of the material makes it appropriate for a variety of uses from household items to clothing.

INGREDIENTS
- ☐ Mesh heat transfer vinyl
- ☐ Base material, such as 100% cotton burp cloth
- ☐ Cover sheet

EQUIPMENT
- ☐ Lint roller
- ☐ Weeding tool
- ☐ Flat heat source such as a heat press

PREPARATION

Start with a new cotton item, such as a burp cloth, for the best results. No need to pre-wash, but if you do, avoid fabric softener.

Pre-heat your flat heat press to the temperature shown in chart below.

Place the vinyl with the carrier sheet side facing down on a machine mat and then use your cutting machine to **cut your desired pattern out of the vinyl. Weed as necessary** to remove any excess vinyl from the design.

Place your cotton material on top of the pressing pad.

Pre-press for 5 seconds to remove moisture and ensure that the burp cloth is wrinkle free.

Place the vinyl on the cotton material with the carrier sheet facing up.

Place a cover sheet on top of the carrier sheet.

Press according to the chart below.

Once you have applied the appropriate amount of heat and pressure, you can **slowly peel away your carrier sheet once it is cool to the touch.**

If your vinyl peels away from the cotton material, carefully replace carrier sheet and apply a little more heat and pressure.

Stack (top to bottom): heat source / cover sheet / HTV with carrier sheet side up / cotton / pressing pad / work surface

COOL PEEL

COOK TIMES
Here are typical times you can use as a starting point. Always check the manufacturer's instructions for time and temperature, when available.

your favorite settings

Traditional Heat Press	AutoPress	EasyPress	Mini Press	
315°F / 157°C	315°F / 157°C	315°F / 157°C	Medium	
30 seconds	40 seconds	30 seconds	25 sec then flip +15 sec	
50 psi (Firm pressure)	Auto pressure	Firm pressure	Firm pressure	

TIPS & TRICKS
- ✗ Do not wash your item for at least 24 hours after applying the HTV. If you wash a garment, turn it inside out first.
- ✓ Remember to mirror your design if it contains words or phrases.

MESH HTV

COTTON/POLY BLEND

Tank top, blanket, burp cloth, dress, hoodie, infant bodysuit, long-sleeved shirt, lounge pants, pajamas, pillowcase, plushie, polo shirt, shorts, sweatshirt, t-shirt

Cotton blends, often found as 50/50 cotton/polyester, of any color are a popular base material for standard heat transfer vinyl. The vinyl can be applied anywhere on the shirt.

INGREDIENTS
- ☐ Mesh heat transfer vinyl
- ☐ Base material, such as cotton blend T-shirt
- ☐ Cover sheet

EQUIPMENT
- ☐ Lint roller
- ☐ Weeding tool
- ☐ Flat heat source such as a heat press
- ☐ (Optional) T-shirt ruler for placement help
- ☐ (Optional) Pillow or foam insert

PREPARATION

Start with a new cotton/polyester blend item, such as a tank top, for the best results. No need to pre-wash, but if you do, avoid fabric softener.

Pre-heat your flat heat press to the temperature shown in chart below.

Place the vinyl with the carrier sheet side facing down on a machine mat and then use your cutting machine to **cut your desired pattern out of the vinyl. Weed as necessary** to remove any excess vinyl from the design.

Use a lint roller to remove any dust or fibers from the cotton/poly blend material.

If you're pressing a shirt, fold the shirt in half lengthwise so both sides match up, then **press for 5 seconds** — this both pre-heats the shirt to remove moisture and gives you a straight vertical crease for alignment.

Unfold the cotton/poly blend material **and lay it flat.** Optionally, slide a pressing pillow or foam insert inside the tank top to provide additional support.

Place the vinyl on the cotton/poly blend material **with the carrier sheet facing up.**

Cover the carrier sheet and vinyl with a cover sheet in order to help avoid overheating the vinyl.

Press according to the chart below.

Let cool, then slowly peel away the carrier sheet. If the vinyl peels away from the cotton/poly blend material, carefully replace the carrier sheet and apply a little more heat and pressure for a short amount of time.

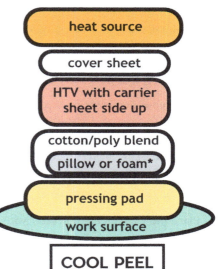

* optional

COOK TIMES
Here are typical times you can use as a starting point. Always check the manufacturer's instructions for time and temperature, when available.

your favorite settings

Traditional Heat Press	AutoPress	EasyPress	Mini Press	
315°F / 157°C	315°F / 157°C	315°F / 157°C	Medium	
30 seconds	40 seconds	30 seconds	25 sec then flip +15 sec	
50 psi (Firm pressure)	Auto pressure	Firm pressure	Firm pressure	

TIPS & TRICKS
- ✗ Do not wash your item for at least 24 hours after applying the HTV. If you wash a garment, turn it inside out first.
- ✓ Remember to mirror your design if it contains words or phrases.

MESH HTV

POLYESTER

Polo shirt, backpack, blanket, dress, hoodie, infant bodysuit, long-sleeved shirt, lounge pants, pajamas, pillowcase, plushie, shorts, tank top, t-shirt

Polyester is a blend of synthetic materials and is one of the most commonly used materials for textiles. Heat transfer vinyl is easily applied with low heat and medium to firm pressure.

INGREDIENTS
- ☐ Mesh heat transfer vinyl
- ☐ Base material, such as polyester polo shirt
- ☐ Cover sheet

EQUIPMENT
- ☐ Weeding tool
- ☐ Lint roller
- ☐ Flat heat source such as a heat press
- ☐ Pressing foam or insert
- ☐ (Optional) T-shirt ruler for placement help

PREPARATION

Start with a new polyester item, such as a polo shirt, for the best results. No need to pre-wash, but if you do, avoid fabric softener.

Pre-heat your flat heat press to the temperature listed below.

Place the vinyl with the carrier sheet side facing down on a machine mat and then use your cutting machine to **cut your desired pattern out of the vinyl. Weed as necessary** to remove any excess vinyl from the design.

Place your polyester on top of the pressing pad.

If you're pressing a shirt, fold the shirt in half lengthwise so both sides match up, then **press for 5 seconds** — this both pre-heats the shirt to remove moisture and gives you a straight vertical crease for alignment.

Unfold the polyester. Optionally, slide a pressing pillow or foam insert inside the shirt to provide additional support.

Place the vinyl on the polyester with the carrier sheet facing up.

Place a piece a cover sheet over the carrier sheet.

Press according to the chart below.

Flip the shirt over and apply additional heat for 15 seconds to the back side.

Allow to cool, then **slowly peel away your carrier sheet.**

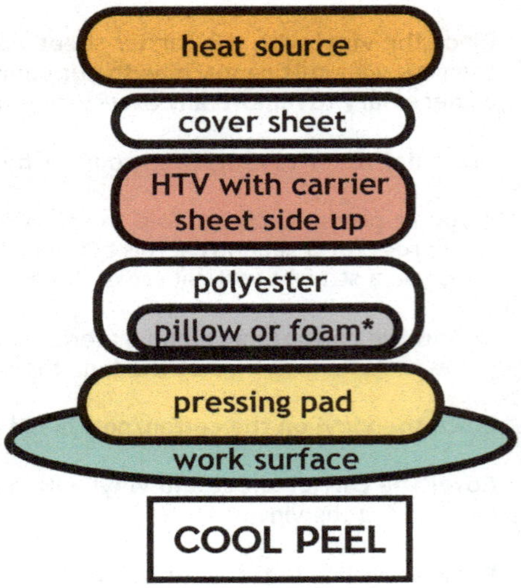

Stack (top to bottom):
- heat source
- cover sheet
- HTV with carrier sheet side up
- polyester
- pillow or foam*
- pressing pad
- work surface

COOL PEEL

* optional

COOK TIMES
Here are typical times you can use as a starting point. Always check the manufacturer's instructions for time and temperature, when available.

Traditional Heat Press	AutoPress	EasyPress	Mini Press	your favorite settings
315°F / 157°C	315°F / 157°C	315°F / 157°C	Medium	
30 seconds	30 seconds	30 seconds	25 seconds	
50 psi (Firm pressure)	Auto pressure	Firm pressure	Firm pressure	

TIPS & TRICKS
× Do not wash your item for at least 24 hours after applying the HTV. If you wash a garment, turn it inside out first.

MESH HTV

WOOD

Cutting board, door sign, crate, doorknob hanger, sign, yard sign, charcuterie board

Wood comes in a variety of finishes and can be painted or stained. Wood can be used both as flat panels and in the construction of 3D objects, such as crates.

INGREDIENTS
☐ Mesh heat transfer vinyl
☐ Base material, such as unfinished wood cutting board
☐ Cover sheet
☐ (Optional) Sandpaper

EQUIPMENT
☐ Microfiber cloth
☐ Weeding tool
☐ Scraper
☐ Flat heat source such as a heat press
☐ (Optional) Heat-resistant tape

PREPARATION

Start with a new wood item, such as a cutting board, for the best results.

Start by prepping your wood cutting board. Optionally, gently sand the surface to remove any wood splinters and wipe with a microfiber cloth to remove any dust and debris. You can also choose to add varnish or paint your wood; however, wait for item to fully dry before applying the HTV.

Pre-heat your flat heat press to the temperature shown in chart below.

Place the vinyl with the carrier sheet side facing down on a machine mat and then use your cutting machine to **cut your desired pattern out of the vinyl. Weed as necessary** to remove any excess vinyl from the design.

Place your wood on the pressing pad and **pre-press it for 5 seconds.**

Place the vinyl on the wood with the carrier sheet facing up.

Optionally, secure the design in place with heat-resistant tape to prevent it from moving.

Cover the carrier sheet with a cover sheet.

Press according to the chart below.

When it's cool, **gently peel away the carrier sheet.**

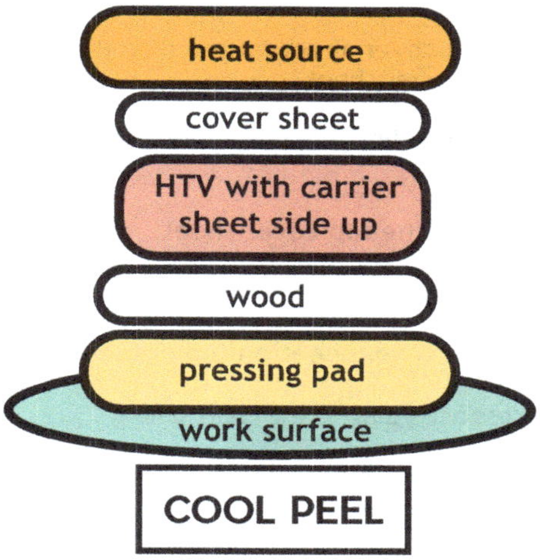

If some parts of the vinyl start lifting off, replace the liner, heat the area for a few seconds, and use your scraper to press the hot vinyl into the wood. Then peel away the carrier sheet.

Stack diagram (top to bottom): heat source / cover sheet / HTV with carrier sheet side up / wood / pressing pad / work surface

COOL PEEL

COOK TIMES
Here are typical times you can use as a starting point. Always check the manufacturer's instructions for time and temperature, when available.

Traditional Heat Press	AutoPress	EasyPress	Mini Press	your favorite settings
300°F / 149°C	300°F / 149°C	300°F / 149°C	Medium	
40 seconds	40 seconds	40 seconds	40 seconds	
50 psi (Firm pressure)	Auto pressure	Firm pressure	Firm pressure	

TIPS & TRICKS
✗ Do not use cleaning products on surface for at least 24 hours after application of the HTV, then use gentle dish soap.
✓ Remember to mirror your design if it contains words or phrases.

MESH HTV

NEOPRENE

Kneeling pad, chapstick holder, coaster, drink sleeve, flip flops, laptop sleeve, lunch bag, mousepad, sanitizer bottle holder

Neoprene is a synthetic rubber material that is often used for insulation of heated or cooled items.

INGREDIENTS
☐ Mesh heat transfer vinyl
☐ Base material, such as neoprene kneeling pad
☐ Cover sheets

EQUIPMENT
☐ Lint roller
☐ Weeding tool
☐ Flat heat source such as a heat press

PREPARATION

Start with a new neoprene item, such as a kneeling pad.

Use a lint roller if necessary to remove dust and debris.

Pre-heat your flat heat press to the temperature shown in chart below.

Place the vinyl with the carrier sheet side facing down on a machine mat and then use your cutting machine to **cut your desired pattern out of the vinyl. Weed as necessary** to remove any excess vinyl from the design.

Place a cover sheet on top of your pressing pad. **Place the neoprene on top** of the cover sheet.

Place another piece of cover sheet on top of the neoprene and **pre-press for 5 seconds.**

Remove the top cover sheet.

Place the vinyl on the neoprene with the carrier sheet facing up.

Place a cover sheet on top of the vinyl carrier sheet.

Press according to the chart below.

Once the item has cooled, **slowly remove the carrier sheet.** If your vinyl peels away from the neoprene, carefully replace carrier sheet and apply a little more heat and pressure.

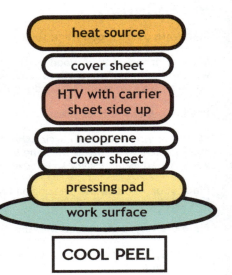

COOK TIMES
Here are typical times you can use as a starting point. Always check the manufacturer's instructions for time and temperature, when available.

Traditional Heat Press	AutoPress	EasyPress	Mini Press	your favorite settings
280°F / 138°C	280°F / 138°C	280°F / 138°C	Medium	
15 seconds	15 seconds	20 seconds	20 seconds	
40 psi (Medium pressure)	Auto pressure	Firm pressure	Firm pressure	

TIPS & TRICKS
✗ Do not wash your item for at least 24 hours after applying the HTV.
✓ Remember to mirror your design if it contains words or phrases.

HOLOGRAPHIC HTV

CHAPTER 4
HOLOGRAPHIC HTV

HOLOGRAPHIC HTV

POLYESTER

T-shirt, backpack, blanket, dress, hoodie, infant bodysuit, long-sleeved shirt, lounge pants, pajamas, pillowcase, plushie, polo shirt, shorts, tank top

Polyester is a blend of synthetic materials and is one of the most commonly used materials for textiles. Heat transfer vinyl is easily applied with low heat and medium to firm pressure.

INGREDIENTS
☐ Holographic heat transfer vinyl
☐ Base material, such as polyester T-shirt
☐ Cover sheet

EQUIPMENT
☐ Lint roller
☐ Weeding tool
☐ Flat heat source such as a heat press
☐ (Optional) T-shirt ruler for placement help
☐ (Optional) Pillow or foam insert

PREPARATION

Start with a new polyester item, such as a shirt, for the best results. No need to pre-wash, but if you do, avoid fabric softener. **Use a lint roller** to remove any dust or fibers from the polyester.

Pre-heat your flat **heat press** to the temperature shown in chart below.

Place the vinyl with the carrier sheet side facing down on a machine mat and then use your cutting machine to **cut your desired pattern out of the vinyl. Weed as necessary** to remove any excess vinyl from the design.

If you're pressing a shirt, **fold the shirt in half lengthwise** so both sides match up, then **press for 5 seconds** — this both pre-heats the shirt to remove moisture and gives you a straight vertical crease for alignment.

Unfold the polyester material and lay it flat. Optionally, slide a pressing pillow inside the shirt to provide additional support.

Place the vinyl on the polyester with the carrier sheet facing up.

Cover the carrier sheet and vinyl with a cover sheet to help avoid overheating the vinyl.

Press according to the chart below.

Let cool, then **slowly peel away the carrier sheet.**

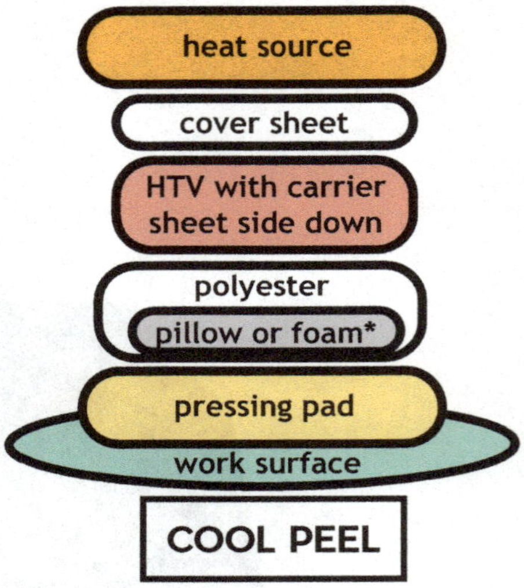

Stack (top to bottom):
- heat source
- cover sheet
- HTV with carrier sheet side down
- polyester
- pillow or foam*
- pressing pad
- work surface

COOL PEEL

* optional

COOK TIMES
Here are typical times you can use as a starting point. Always check the manufacturer's instructions for time and temperature, when available.

your favorite settings

Traditional Heat Press	AutoPress	EasyPress	Mini Press	
330°F / 166°C	330°F / 166°C	330°F / 166°C	Medium	
30 seconds	30 seconds	30 seconds	25 sec then flip +15 sec	
50 psi (Firm pressure)	Auto pressure	Firm pressure	Firm pressure	

TIPS & TRICKS
✓ Check out a tutorial at jennifermaker.com/cricut-vinyl-projects
✗ Do not wash your item for at least 24 hours after applying the HTV. If you wash a garment, turn it inside out first.

HOLOGRAPHIC HTV

COTTON

Hoodie, blanket, burp cloth, denim, dress, infant bodysuit, long-sleeved shirt, lounge pants, pajamas, pillowcase, plushie, polo shirt, shorts, sweatshirt, tank top, t-shirt

Items made from 100% cotton work well for heat transfer vinyl. The versatility of the material makes it appropriate for a variety of uses from household items to clothing.

INGREDIENTS
☐ Holographic heat transfer vinyl
☐ Base material, such as cotton hoodie
☐ Cover sheet

EQUIPMENT
☐ Lint roller
☐ Weeding tool
☐ Flat heat source such as a heat press
☐ (Optional) T-shirt ruler for placement help
☐ (Optional) Pillow or foam insert

PREPARATION

Start with a new cotton item, such as a hoodie. No need to pre-wash, but if you do, avoid fabric softener.

Pre-heat your flat heat press to the temperature shown in chart below.

Place the vinyl with the carrier sheet side facing down on a machine mat and then use your cutting machine to **cut your desired pattern out of the vinyl. Weed as necessary** to remove any excess vinyl from the design.

Use a lint roller to remove any dust or fibers from the cotton material.

If you're pressing a shirt, fold the shirt in half lengthwise so both sides match up, then **press for 5 seconds** — this both pre-heats the shirt to remove moisture and gives you a straight vertical crease for alignment.

Unfold the cotton material and lay it flat. Optionally, slide a pressing pillow inside to provide additional support.

Place the vinyl on the cotton material with the carrier sheet facing up. Cover the carrier sheet and vinyl with a cover sheet to help avoid overheating the vinyl.

Press according to the chart below. Keep the hoodie strings out of the way.

Let cool, then slowly peel away the carrier sheet. If the vinyl peels away from the cotton material, carefully replace the carrier sheet and apply a little more heat and pressure for a short amount of time.

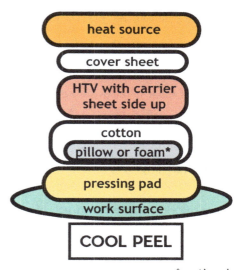

optional

COOK TIMES
Here are typical times you can use as a starting point. Always check the manufacturer's instructions for time and temperature, when available.

your favorite settings

Traditional Heat Press	AutoPress	EasyPress	Mini Press	
330°F / 166°C	330°F / 166°C	330°F / 166°C	Medium	
40 seconds	45 seconds	30 seconds	25 sec then flip +15 sec	
50 psi (Firm pressure)	Auto pressure	Firm pressure	Firm pressure	

TIPS & TRICKS
✗ Do not wash your item for at least 24 hours after applying the HTV. If you wash a garment, turn it inside out first.
✓ Remember to mirror your design if it contains words or phrases.

HOLOGRAPHIC HTV

COTTON/POLY BLEND

Polo shirt, blanket, burp cloth, dress, hoodie, infant bodysuit, long-sleeved shirt, lounge pants, pajamas, pillowcase, plushie, shorts, sweatshirt, tank top, t-shirt

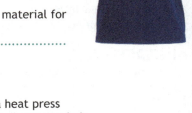

Cotton blends, often found as 50/50 cotton/polyester, of any color are a popular base material for holographic heat transfer vinyl. The vinyl can be applied anywhere on the shirt.

INGREDIENTS
☐ Holographic heat transfer vinyl
☐ Base material, such as cotton/poly blend polo shirt
☐ Cover sheet

EQUIPMENT
☐ Lint roller
☐ Weeding tool
☐ Flat heat source such as a heat press
☐ (Optional) T-shirt ruler for placement help
☐ (Optional) Pillow or foam insert

PREPARATION

Start with a new cotton/polyester blend item, such as a polo shirt, for the best results. No need to pre-wash, but if you do, avoid fabric softener.

Pre-heat your flat heat press to the temperature shown in chart below.

Place the vinyl with the carrier sheet side facing down on a machine mat and then use your cutting machine to **cut your desired pattern out of the vinyl. Weed as necessary** to remove any excess vinyl from the design.

Use a lint roller to remove any dust or fibers from the cotton/poly blend material.

If you're pressing a shirt, fold the shirt in half lengthwise so both sides match up, then **press for 5 seconds** — this both pre-heats the shirt to remove moisture and gives you a straight vertical crease for alignment.

Unfold the cotton/poly blend material **and lay it flat.** Optionally, slide a pressing pillow inside to provide additional support.

Place the vinyl on the cotton/poly blend material **with the carrier sheet facing up.**

Cover the carrier sheet and vinyl with a cover sheet in order to help avoid overheating the vinyl.

Press according to the chart below. Take care to avoid pressing any buttons.

Let cool, then slowly peel away the carrier sheet.

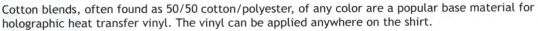

heat source
cover sheet
HTV with carrier sheet side up
cotton/poly blend
pillow or foam*
pressing pad
work surface

COOL PEEL

* optional

COOK TIMES

Here are typical times you can use as a starting point. Always check the manufacturer's instructions for time and temperature, when available.

your favorite settings

Traditional Heat Press	AutoPress	EasyPress	Mini Press	
330°F / 166°C	330°F / 166°C	330°F / 166°C	Medium	
30 seconds	30 seconds	30 seconds	25 sec then flip +15 sec	
50 psi (Firm pressure)	Auto pressure	Firm pressure	Firm pressure	

TIPS & TRICKS
✓ Check out the tutorial at jennifermaker.com/cricut-vinyl-projects
✗ Do not wash your item for at least 24 hours after applying the HTV. If you wash a garment, turn it inside out first.

HOLOGRAPHIC HTV

CANVAS

Tote bag, art canvas, backdrop, cooler, flag, reverse art canvas, placemat, sail, shoes, tent

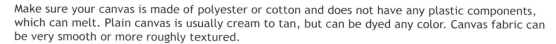

Make sure your canvas is made of polyester or cotton and does not have any plastic components, which can melt. Plain canvas is usually cream to tan, but can be dyed any color. Canvas fabric can be very smooth or more roughly textured.

INGREDIENTS
- ☐ Holographic heat transfer vinyl
- ☐ Base material, such as canvas tote bag
- ☐ Cover sheet

EQUIPMENT
- ☐ Lint roller
- ☐ Weeding tool
- ☐ Flat heat source such as a heat press
- ☐ (Optional) Ruler for placement help
- ☐ (Optional) Pillow or foam insert

PREPARATION

Start with a new canvas item, such as a tote bag, for the best results. No need to pre-wash, but if you do, avoid fabric softener.

Pre-heat your flat heat press to the temperature shown in chart below.

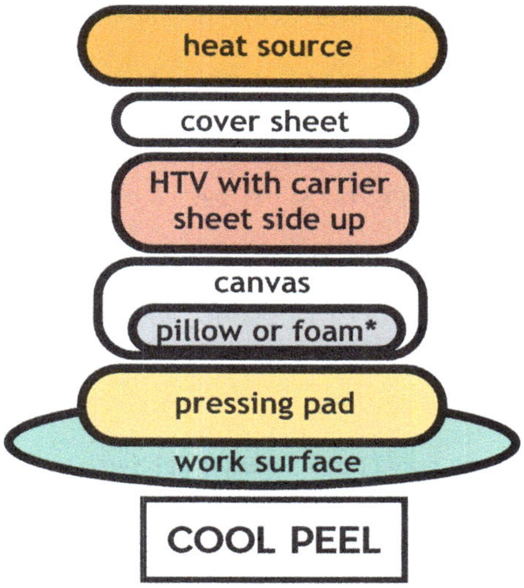

Place the vinyl with the carrier sheet side facing down on a machine mat and then use your cutting machine to **cut your desired pattern out of the vinyl. Weed as necessary** to remove any excess vinyl from the design.

Use a lint roller to remove any dust or fibers from the canvas.

Fold the canvas in half lengthwise so both sides match up, then **press for 10 seconds** — this both pre-heats the canvas to remove moisture and gives you a straight vertical crease for alignment.

Unfold the canvas and lay it flat. Optionally, slide a pressing pillow inside the tote bag to provide additional support.

Place the vinyl on the canvas with the carrier sheet facing up.

Cover the carrier sheet and vinyl with a cover sheet to help avoid overheating the vinyl.

Press according to the chart below.

Let cool, then slowly peel away the carrier sheet. If the vinyl peels away from the canvas, carefully replace the carrier sheet and apply a little more heat and pressure for a short amount of time.

Stack (top to bottom):
- heat source
- cover sheet
- HTV with carrier sheet side up
- canvas
- pillow or foam*
- pressing pad
- work surface

COOL PEEL

*optional

COOK TIMES

Here are typical times you can use as a starting point. Always check the manufacturer's instructions for time and temperature, when available.

your favorite settings

Traditional Heat Press	AutoPress	EasyPress	Mini Press	
285°F / 141°C	285°F / 141°C	285°F / 141°C	Low	
20 seconds	15 seconds	30 seconds	35 seconds	
50 psi (Firm pressure)	Auto pressure	Firm pressure	Firm pressure	

TIPS & TRICKS
- ✓ Check out a tutorial at jennifermaker.com/cricut-vinyl-projects
- ✗ Do not wash your item for at least 24 hours after applying the HTV. If possible, turn item inside out before washing.

HOLOGRAPHIC HTV

FAUX LEATHER

Journal cover, baggage tag, bookmark, cosmetic bag, earrings, notebook, tote bag, wallet

Faux leather is a synthetic plastic-based material used to mimic the look of real leather. It is available in a variety of colors and patterns and is often used for accessories rather than apparel.

INGREDIENTS
- ☐ Holographic heat transfer vinyl
- ☐ Base material, such as faux leather journal
- ☐ Cover sheet

EQUIPMENT
- ☐ Microfiber cloth
- ☐ Weeding tool
- ☐ Flat heat source such as a heat press
- ☐ (Optional) Ruler for placement help

PREPARATION

Start with a new faux leather item, such as a journal, for the best results.

Pre-heat your flat heat press to the temperature shown in chart below.

Place the vinyl with the carrier sheet side facing down on a machine mat and then use your cutting machine to **cut your desired pattern out of the vinyl. Weed as necessary** to remove any excess vinyl from the design.

Use a microfiber cloth to remove any dust or debris from the faux leather.

Place a cover sheet over the faux leather and pre-press for 5 seconds.

Place the vinyl on the faux leather with the carrier sheet facing up.

Cover the carrier sheet and vinyl with a cover sheet to help avoid overheating the vinyl or melting the faux leather.

Press according to the chart below.

Let cool, then slowly peel away the carrier sheet. If the vinyl peels away from the faux leather, carefully replace the carrier sheet and apply a little more heat and pressure for a short amount of time.

Layers (top to bottom):
- heat source
- cover sheet
- HTV with carrier sheet side up
- faux leather
- pressing pad
- work surface

COOL PEEL

COOK TIMES
Here are typical times you can use as a starting point. Always check the manufacturer's instructions for time and temperature, when available.

your favorite settings

Traditional Heat Press	AutoPress	EasyPress	Mini Press	
285°F / 141°C	285°F / 141°C	285°F / 141°C	Low	
15 seconds	15 seconds	30 seconds	30 seconds	
50 psi (Firm pressure)	Auto pressure	Firm pressure	Firm pressure	

TIPS & TRICKS
- ✗ Do not raise the pressing temperature. This risks melting the faux leather.
- ✓ Remember to mirror your design if it contains words or phrases.

HOLOGRAPHIC HTV

BURLAP

Pillowcase, bag, banner, bunting, garden flag, table runner, wine bag, wreath

Burlap is a material made of plant fibers. Natural burlap comes in shades of brown, but it can be dyed any color. Burlap fabric is textured and can be tightly or loosely woven.

INGREDIENTS
- ☐ Holographic heat transfer vinyl
- ☐ Base material, such as burlap pillowcase
- ☐ Cover sheet

EQUIPMENT
- ☐ Lint roller
- ☐ Weeding tool
- ☐ Flat heat source such as a heat press
- ☐ (Optional) Ruler for placement help

PREPARATION

Start with a new burlap item, such as a pillowcase, for the best results.

Pre-heat your flat heat press to the temperature shown in chart below.

Place the vinyl with the carrier sheet side facing down on a machine mat and then use your cutting machine to **cut your desired pattern out of the vinyl. Weed as necessary** to remove any excess vinyl from the design.

Use a lint roller to remove any dust or loose fibers from the burlap.

Pre-press the burlap for 5 seconds to eliminate any moisture.

Place the vinyl on the burlap with the carrier sheet facing up.

Cover the carrier sheet and vinyl with a cover sheet to help avoid overheating the vinyl.

Press according to the chart below, taking care to avoid any zippers.

Let cool, then slowly peel away the carrier sheet. If the vinyl peels away from the burlap, carefully replace the carrier sheet and apply a little more heat and pressure for a short amount of time.

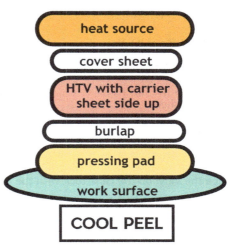

COOK TIMES
Here are typical times you can use as a starting point. Always check the manufacturer's instructions for time and temperature, when available.

Traditional Heat Press	AutoPress	EasyPress	Mini Press	*your favorite settings*
305°F / 152°C	305°F / 152°C	305°F / 152°C	Medium	
15 seconds	15 seconds	30 seconds	30 sec then flip +15 sec	
50 psi (Firm pressure)	Auto pressure	Firm pressure	Firm pressure	

TIPS & TRICKS
- ✓ Remember to mirror your design if it contains words or phrases.
- ✗ Do not wash for at least 24 hours after applying vinyl.

HOLOGRAPHIC HTV

CARDSTOCK
Cardstock folded card, cardboard, notebook cover, notecard

Cardstock comes in almost every color, pattern, and finish you can imagine. It is available both in solid core and white core. It is available is several weights and sizes.

INGREDIENTS
☐ Holographic heat transfer vinyl
☐ Base material, such as cardstock card
☐ Cover sheet

EQUIPMENT
☐ Lint roller
☐ Weeding tool
☐ Flat heat source such as a heat press
☐ (Optional) Ruler for placement help

PREPARATION

Start with a new cardstock item, such as a folded card, for the best results.

Pre-heat your flat heat press to the temperature shown in chart below.

Place the vinyl with the carrier sheet side facing down on a machine mat and then use your cutting machine to **cut your desired pattern out of the vinyl. Weed as necessary** to remove any excess vinyl from the design.

Unfold the cardstock so it lays flat, if necessary.

Gently use the lint roller to clean any dust or debris from the face of the cardstock sheet.

Place the cardstock on a hard surface, such as a wood cutting board or table. **Place a cover sheet** over the cardstock and **pre-press for 5 seconds. Remove the cover sheet.**

Place the vinyl on the cardstock with the carrier sheet facing up.

Cover the carrier sheet and vinyl with a cover sheet to help avoid overheating the vinyl or scorching the cardstock.

Press according to the chart below. Make sure you are pressing on a hard surface so the cardstock does not warp.

Slowly peel away the carrier sheet after it is cool to the touch. If the vinyl peels away from the cardstock sheet, carefully replace the carrier sheet and apply a little more heat and pressure for a short amount of time.

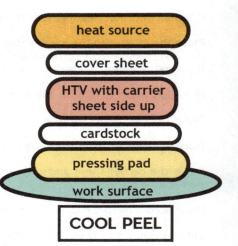

COOK TIMES
Here are typical times you can use as a starting point. Always check the manufacturer's instructions for time and temperature, when available.

your favorite settings

Traditional Heat Press	AutoPress	EasyPress	Mini Press	
290°F / 143°C	290°F / 143°C	290°F / 143°C	Low	
15 seconds	15 seconds	30 seconds	25 seconds	
50 psi (Firm pressure)	Auto pressure	Firm pressure	Firm pressure	

TIPS & TRICKS
✓ Remember to mirror your design if it contains words or phrases.
✓ Wait until the HTV is applied to use markers, glue, and to decorate the card.

HOLOGRAPHIC HTV

WOOD

Cutting board, door sign, crate, doorknob hanger, sign, yard sign, charcuterie board

Wood comes in a variety of finishes and can be painted or stained. Wood can be used both as flat panels and in the construction of 3D objects, such as crates.

INGREDIENTS
- ☐ Holographic heat transfer vinyl
- ☐ Base material, such as unsealed cutting board
- ☐ Cover sheet
- ☐ (Optional) Sandpaper

EQUIPMENT
- ☐ Microfiber cloth
- ☐ Weeding tool
- ☐ Flat heat source such as a heat press
- ☐ (Optional) Ruler for placement help
- ☐ (Optional) Heat-resistant tape

PREPARATION

Start with a new wood item, such as a cutting board, for the best results.

Pre-heat your flat heat press to the temperature shown in chart below.

Place the vinyl with the carrier sheet side facing down on a machine mat and then use your cutting machine to **cut your desired pattern out of the vinyl. Weed as necessary** to remove any excess vinyl from the design.

If desired, **lightly sand the surface of the wood. Use a microfiber cloth** to clean the surface of the wood.

Place a cover sheet over the wood and **pre-press for 5 seconds.**

Place the vinyl on the wood with the carrier sheet facing up.

Optionally, you can secure your design down with heat-resistant tape.

Cover the carrier sheet and vinyl with a cover sheet to help avoid overheating the vinyl.

Press according to the chart below.

Let cool, then slowly peel away the carrier sheet. If the vinyl peels away from the wood, carefully replace the carrier sheet and apply a little more heat and pressure for a short amount of time, then use a scraper to push the vinyl down into place.

Layer stack (top to bottom): heat source / cover sheet / HTV with carrier sheet side up / wood / pressing pad / work surface. **COOL PEEL**

COOK TIMES

Here are typical times you can use as a starting point. Always check the manufacturer's instructions for time and temperature, when available.

your favorite settings

Traditional Heat Press	AutoPress	EasyPress	Mini Press	
300°F / 149°C	300°F / 149°C	300°F / 149°C	Medium	
45 seconds	45 seconds	40 seconds	40 seconds	
50 psi (Firm pressure)	Auto pressure	Firm pressure	Firm pressure	

TIPS & TRICKS
- ✗ Do not use a cutting board for cutting food after applying vinyl.
- ✓ Remember to mirror your design if it contains words or phrases.
- ✓ To clean, use a microfiber cloth to gently wipe away dust.

HOLOGRAPHIC HTV

CORK
Corkboard, coaster, serving tray, trivet, yoga block

Cork is a natural material that is lightweight and water-resistant. It can be flexible or made to be stiff and is usually used in home decor and accessories.

INGREDIENTS
☐ Holographic heat transfer vinyl
☐ Base material, such as corkboard
☐ Cover sheet

EQUIPMENT
☐ Lint roller
☐ Weeding tool
☐ Flat heat source such as a heat press
☐ (Optional) Ruler for placement help

PREPARATION

Start with a new cork item, such as a corkboard, for the best results.

Pre-heat your flat heat press to the temperature shown in chart below.

Place the vinyl with the carrier sheet side facing down on a machine mat and then use your cutting machine to **cut your desired pattern out of the vinyl. Weed as necessary** to remove any excess vinyl from the design.

Use a lint roller to remove any dust or debris from the cork.

Place a cover sheet over the cork and **pre-press for 5 seconds.**

Place the vinyl on the cork with the carrier sheet facing up.

Cover the carrier sheet and vinyl with a cover sheet to help avoid overheating the vinyl.

Press according to the chart below.

Let cool, then slowly peel away the carrier sheet. If the vinyl peels away from the cork, carefully replace the carrier sheet and apply a little more heat and pressure for a short amount of time.

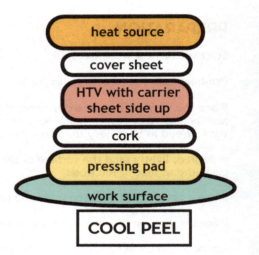

COOK TIMES
Here are typical times you can use as a starting point. Always check the manufacturer's instructions for time and temperature, when available.

Traditional Heat Press	AutoPress	EasyPress	Mini Press	your favorite settings
315°F / 157°C	315°F / 157°C	315°F / 157°C	Medium	
15 seconds	15 seconds	15 seconds	25 seconds	
50 psi (Firm pressure)	Auto pressure	Firm pressure	Firm pressure	

TIPS & TRICKS
✓ Remember to mirror your design if it contains words or phrases.
✓ To clean, use a microfiber cloth to gently wipe away dust.
✓ Once the corkboard has cooled completely, you can insert tacks or key holder pegs.
✓ Check out a tutorial on customized cork coasters here jennifermaker.com/custom-cork-coasters/

HOLOGRAPHIC HTV

NEOPRENE

Laptop sleeve, chapstick holder, coaster, drink sleeve, flip flops, kneeling pad, lunch bag, mousepad, sanitizer bottle holder

Neoprene is a synthetic rubber material that is often used for insulation of heated or cooled items.

INGREDIENTS
- ☐ Holographic heat transfer vinyl
- ☐ Base material, such as laptop sleeve
- ☐ Cover sheets

EQUIPMENT
- ☐ Lint roller
- ☐ Weeding tool
- ☐ Flat heat source such as a heat press
- ☐ (Optional) Ruler for placement help
- ☐ (Optional) Pillow or foam insert

PREPARATION

Start with a new neoprene item, such as a laptop sleeve, for the best results.

Pre-heat your flat heat press to the temperature shown in chart below.

Place the vinyl with the carrier sheet side facing down on a machine mat and then use your cutting machine to **cut your desired pattern out of the vinyl.** **Weed as necessary** to remove any excess vinyl from the design.

Use a lint roller to remove any dust or fibers from the neoprene.

Optionally, slide a pressing pillow or foam insert inside the neoprene to provide additional support.

Place a cover sheet on the pressing pad and **lay the neoprene on top.**

Place a cover sheet over the neoprene and **pre-press for 10 seconds.** Remove the cover sheet.

Place the vinyl on the neoprene with the carrier sheet facing up.

Cover the carrier sheet and vinyl with a cover sheet to help avoid overheating the vinyl.

Press according to the chart below.

Let cool, then slowly peel away the carrier sheet.

Stack (top to bottom): heat source / cover sheet / HTV with carrier sheet side up / neoprene / pillow or foam* / pressing pad / work surface

COOL PEEL

optional

COOK TIMES
Here are typical times you can use as a starting point. Always check the manufacturer's instructions for time and temperature, when available.

your favorite settings

Traditional Heat Press	AutoPress	EasyPress	Mini Press	
280°F / 138°C	280°F / 138°C	280°F / 138°C	Medium	
15 seconds	15 seconds	20 seconds	20 seconds	
50 psi (Firm pressure)	Auto pressure	Firm pressure	Firm pressure	

TIPS & TRICKS
- ✓ Take care to avoid pressing the zipper and any handles or straps.
- ✗ Do not wash your item for at least 24 hours after applying the HTV. If possible, turn item inside out before washing.

HOLOGRAPHIC HTV

CERAMIC
Mug, mug without handles, pencil cup

Ceramic is a product formed by clay that has been hardened by high heat. This recipe is for curved ceramic items such as mugs. Mugs with heat transfer vinyl require two heat sources to get the best results.

INGREDIENTS
- ☐ Holographic heat transfer vinyl
- ☐ Base material, such as ceramic mug

EQUIPMENT
- ☐ Rubbing alcohol
- ☐ Microfiber cloth
- ☐ Heat-resistant gloves
- ☐ Heat-resistant tape
- ☐ Oven-safe tray
- ☐ Weeding tool
- ☐ Mini Press
- ☐ Oven

PREPARATION

Start with a new ceramic item, such as a mug, for the best results.

Pre-heat your mini press and oven to the temperatures shown in the chart below.

Use the rubbing alcohol and microfiber cloth to gently clean the outside surface of the ceramic. Let dry completely.

Place the vinyl with the carrier sheet side facing down on a machine mat and then use your cutting machine to **cut your desired pattern out of the vinyl. Weed as necessary** to remove any excess vinyl from the design.

Place the vinyl on the ceramic with the carrier sheet facing up.

Use the mini press according to the chart below to press each section or letter of your design.

Let cool, then **slowly peel the carrier sheet away.**

Place the ceramic on an oven-safe tray and place both in your oven according to the chart below.

Once time is up, **use oven mitts to remove the tray and ceramic from the oven.** Let cool completely.

Stack (top to bottom): mini press / HTV with carrier sheet side up / ceramic / work surface

COOL PEEL

COOK TIMES
Here are typical times you can use as a starting point. Always check the manufacturer's instructions for time and temperature, when available.

Mini Press		Oven	*your favorite settings*
High		300°F / 149°C	
30 seconds	THEN	15 minutes	
Medium pressure			

TIPS & TRICKS
- ✓ Mugs with heat transfer vinyl applied are dishwasher safe. Wash in the top rack on normal cycle.
- ✓ Your household oven is safe to use for this project. You can also use a tabletop convection or toaster oven.
- ✓ Check out the "Iron On Vinyl" section of my tutorial at jennifermaker.com/best-cricut-vinyl-for-coffee-mugs

CHAPTER 5
GLITTER HTV

GLITTER HTV

COTTON

Zip-up hoodie, blanket, burp cloth, denim, dress, infant bodysuit, long-sleeved shirt, lounge pants, pajamas, pillowcase, plushie, polo shirt, shorts, sweatshirt, tank top, t-shirt

Items made from 100% cotton work well for heat transfer vinyl. The versatility of the material makes it appropriate for a variety of uses from household items to clothing.

INGREDIENTS
- ☐ Glitter heat transfer vinyl
- ☐ Base material, such as 100% cotton zip up hoodie
- ☐ Cover sheet

EQUIPMENT
- ☐ Lint roller
- ☐ Weeding tool
- ☐ Flat heat source such as a heat press
- ☐ (Optional) Pressing pillow or foam

PREPARATION

Start with a new cotton item, such as a zip up hoodie, for the best results. No need to pre-wash, but if you do, avoid fabric softener.

Pre-heat your flat heat press to the temperature shown in chart below.

Place the vinyl with the glitter side down on the machine mat with the dull side facing up and then use your cutting machine to **cut your desired pattern out of the vinyl. Weed as necessary** to remove any excess vinyl from the design.

Place your cotton material on top of the pressing pad.

Use the lint roller to clean any dust, debris, or loose fibers on the cotton material.

If you're pressing a shirt, fold the shirt in half lengthwise so both sides match up, then **press for 5 seconds** — this both pre-heats the shirt to remove moisture and gives you a straight vertical crease for alignment.

Optionally, unfold the cotton material and **slide a pressing pillow inside.**

Place the vinyl on the cotton material with the carrier sheet facing up.

Place a cover sheet over the carrier sheet and vinyl.

Press according to the chart below.

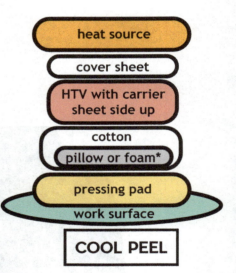

*optional

Flip the cotton material over and apply additional heat for **15 seconds to the back side of the design.**

Once you have applied the appropriate amount of heat and pressure, and the carrier sheet is cool to the touch, **slowly peel away your carrier sheet.** If your vinyl peels away from the cotton material, carefully replace carrier sheet and apply a little more heat and pressure.

COOK TIMES
Here are typical times you can use as a starting point. Always check the manufacturer's instructions for time and temperature, when available.

your favorite settings

Traditional Heat Press	AutoPress	EasyPress	Mini Press	
330°F / 166°C	330°F / 166°C	330°F / 166°C	Medium	
30 seconds	30 seconds	30 seconds	25 seconds	
50 psi (Firm pressure)	Auto pressure	Firm pressure	Firm pressure	

TIPS & TRICKS
× Do not wash your item for at least 24 hours after applying the HTV. If you wash a garment, turn it inside out first.

GLITTER HTV

POLYESTER

Blanket, backpack, dress, hoodie, infant bodysuit, long-sleeved shirt, lounge pants, pajamas, pillowcase, plushie, polo shirt, shorts, tank top, t-shirt

Polyester is a blend of synthetic materials and is one of the most commonly used materials for textiles. Heat transfer vinyl is easily applied with low heat and medium to firm pressure.

INGREDIENTS
☐ Glitter heat transfer vinyl
☐ Base material, such as polyester blanket
☐ Cover sheet

EQUIPMENT
☐ Weeding tool
☐ Lint roller
☐ Flat heat source such as a heat press
☐ (Optional) Ruler for placement help

PREPARATION

Start with a new polyester item, such as a blanket, for the best results. No need to pre-wash, but if you do, avoid fabric softener.

Pre-heat your flat heat press to the temperature listed below.

Place the vinyl with the glitter side down on the machine mat with the dull side facing up. Then use your cutting machine to **cut your desired pattern out of the vinyl.** Weed as necessary to remove any excess vinyl from the design.

Place the section of polyester material that you plan to apply the design to on top of the pressing pad. **Pre-press for 10 seconds.**

Place the vinyl on the polyester material with the carrier sheet facing up.

Place a cover sheet over the carrier sheet and vinyl to avoid overheating the vinyl.

Press according to the chart below.

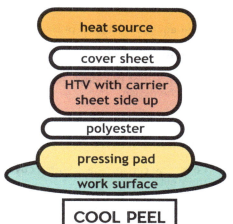

Once you have applied the appropriate amount of heat and pressure, let cool to the touch.
Then, **slowly peel away your carrier sheet.** If your vinyl peels away from the polyester material, carefully replace carrier sheet and apply a little more heat and pressure.

COOK TIMES

Here are typical times you can use as a starting point. Always check the manufacturer's instructions for time and temperature, when available.

your favorite settings

Traditional Heat Press	AutoPress	EasyPress	Mini Press	
330°F / 166°C	330°F / 166°C	330°F / 166°C	Medium	
30 seconds	30 seconds	30 seconds	25 sec then flip +15 sec	
50 psi (Firm pressure)	Auto pressure	Firm pressure	Firm pressure	

TIPS & TRICKS

✗ Do not wash your item for at least 24 hours after applying the HTV. If you wash a garment, turn it inside out first.
✓ Don't forget to mirror your design if your design has words or phrases.
✓ For larger designs, you can tile the work and heat small sections at a time.
✓ For a tutorial on how to make larger-than-mat designs, check out jennifermaker.com/large-wall-decal-larger-than-mat-cricut

GLITTER HTV

CANVAS

Zipper pouch, backdrop, cooler, flag, reverse art canvas, placemat, sail, shoes, tent, tote bag

Make sure your canvas is made of polyester or cotton and does not have any plastic components, which can melt. Plain canvas is usually cream to tan, but can be dyed any color. Canvas fabric can be very smooth or more roughly textured.

INGREDIENTS
- ☐ Glitter heat transfer vinyl
- ☐ Base material, such as canvas zipper pouch
- ☐ Cover sheet

EQUIPMENT
- ☐ Lint roller
- ☐ Weeding tool
- ☐ Flat heat source such as a heat press
- ☐ (Optional) Ruler for placement help
- ☐ (Optional) Pressing pillow or foam

PREPARATION

Start with a new canvas item, such as a blank zipper pouch.

Pre-heat your flat heat press to the temperature shown in chart below.

Place the vinyl with the glitter side down on the machine mat with the dull side facing up. Then use your cutting machine to **cut your desired pattern out of the vinyl. Weed as necessary** to remove any excess vinyl from the design.

Place your canvas on top of the pressing pad. **Pre-press for 5 seconds.**

Place the vinyl on the canvas with the carrier sheet facing up.

Cover the carrier sheet with a cover sheet to help avoid overheating the vinyl.

Press according to the chart below.

Once you have applied the appropriate amount of heat and pressure, allow the canvas to cool before you **slowly peel away your carrier sheet.**

If your vinyl peels away from the canvas, carefully replace carrier sheet and apply a little more heat and pressure.

Stack (top to bottom): heat source, cover sheet, HTV with carrier sheet side up, canvas, pillow or foam*, pressing pad, work surface. **COOL PEEL** *optional

COOK TIMES

Here are typical times you can use as a starting point. Always check the manufacturer's instructions for time and temperature, when available.

Traditional Heat Press	AutoPress	EasyPress	Mini Press	your favorite settings
340°F / 171°C	320°F / 160°C	270°F / 132°C	Medium	
25 seconds	15 seconds	30 seconds	25 seconds	
50 psi (Firm pressure)	Auto pressure	Firm pressure	Firm pressure	

TIPS & TRICKS

- ✗ Do not wash your item for at least 24 hours after applying the HTV. If possible, turn item inside out before washing.
- ✓ Remember to mirror your design if it contains words or phrases.
- ✓ Check out a tutorial of applying HTV to a canvas cosmetic bag at jennifermaker.com/cricut-vinyl-projects

GLITTER HTV

GLASS
Glass block, drinking glass, jar candle, pane, panel, plaque, vase

Since glass is a conductor of heat, it is an easy material to apply heat transfer vinyl to. You can apply to a variety of glass surfaces using caution as it does heat quickly and can be fragile.

INGREDIENTS
- ☐ Glitter heat transfer vinyl
- ☐ Base material, such as glass block
- ☐ Cover sheet

EQUIPMENT
- ☐ Microfiber cloth
- ☐ Rubbing alcohol
- ☐ Weeding tool
- ☐ Heat-resistant gloves
- ☐ Flat heat source such as a heat press

PREPARATION

Start with a new glass item, such as a glass block, for the best results.

Pre-heat your flat heat press to the temperature shown in chart below.

Place the vinyl with the glitter side down on the machine mat with the dull side facing up. Then use your cutting machine to **cut your desired pattern out of the vinyl. Weed as necessary** to remove any excess vinyl from the design.

Use a microfiber cloth and rubbing alcohol to clean the face of your glass. Let dry completely.

Place the vinyl on the glass with the carrier sheet facing up.

Cover the carrier sheet and vinyl with a cover sheet to help avoid overheating the vinyl and the glass.

Press according to the chart below.

Let cool, then **slowly peel away the carrier sheet**.

If the vinyl peels away from the glass, carefully replace the carrier sheet and apply a little more heat and pressure for a short amount of time.

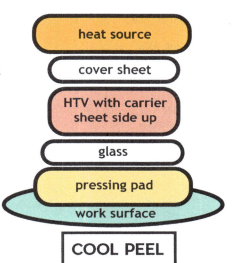

COOK TIMES
Here are typical times you can use as a starting point. Always check the manufacturer's instructions for time and temperature, when available.

your favorite settings

Traditional Heat Press	AutoPress	EasyPress	Mini Press	
315°F / 157°C	315°F / 157°C	315°F / 157°C	Medium	
15 seconds	15 seconds	15 seconds	15 seconds	
30 psi (Light pressure)	Auto pressure	Light pressure	Light pressure	

TIPS & TRICKS
- ✓ Remember to mirror your design if it contains words or phrases.
- ✓ Using a Mini Press is recommended to work around the curve of any curved glass blank. Do NOT use a traditional heat press or Autopress for glass blanks with curved surfaces.
- ✗ Use caution when using a flat press to apply heat to any curved surface.

GLITTER HTV

METAL

License plate, baking tray, bin, bucket, keychain, license plate cover, lunchbox, sheet metal, sign, tumbler

Heat transfer vinyl will adhere to most metal surfaces. Pay particular attention to heat safety when applying as metal is a conductor of heat.

INGREDIENTS
☐ Glitter heat transfer vinyl
☐ Base material, such as metal license plate
☐ Cover sheet

EQUIPMENT
☐ Microfiber cloth
☐ Rubbing alcohol
☐ Weeding tool
☐ Flat heat source such as a heat press
☐ Heat-resistant gloves
☐ (Optional) Ruler for placement help

PREPARATION

Start with a new metal item, such as a license plate, for the best results.

Pre-heat your flat heat press to the temperature shown in chart below.

Use a microfiber cloth and rubbing alcohol to clean the face of your metal. Let dry completely.

Place the vinyl with the glitter side down on the machine mat with the dull side facing up. Then use your cutting machine to **cut your desired pattern out of the vinyl. Weed as necessary** to remove any excess vinyl from the design.

Place the vinyl on the metal with the carrier sheet facing up.

Cover the carrier sheet and vinyl with a cover sheet to help avoid overheating the vinyl.

Press according to the chart below.

Let cool, then **slowly peel away the carrier sheet.** If the vinyl peels away from the metal, carefully replace the carrier sheet and apply a little more heat and pressure for a short amount of time.

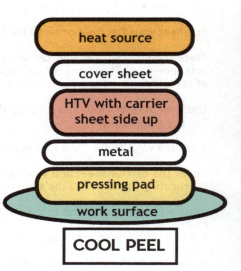

COOL PEEL

COOK TIMES
Here are typical times you can use as a starting point. Always check the manufacturer's instructions for time and temperature, when available.

your favorite settings

Traditional Heat Press	AutoPress	EasyPress	Mini Press	
300°F / 149°C	300°F / 149°C	300°F / 149°C	Medium	
15 seconds	15 seconds	15 seconds	20 seconds	
50 psi (Firm pressure)	Auto pressure	Firm pressure	Firm pressure	

TIPS & TRICKS
✓ Remember to mirror your design if it contains words or phrases.
✓ Using a Mini Press is recommended to work around the curve of any curved metal blank. Do NOT use a traditional heat press or AutoPress for metal blanks with surfaces.
✗ Use caution when using a flat press to apply heat to any curved surface.

NEOPRENE

Lunch bag, chapstick holder, coaster, drink sleeve, flip flops, kneeling pad, laptop sleeve, mousepad, sanitizer bottle holder

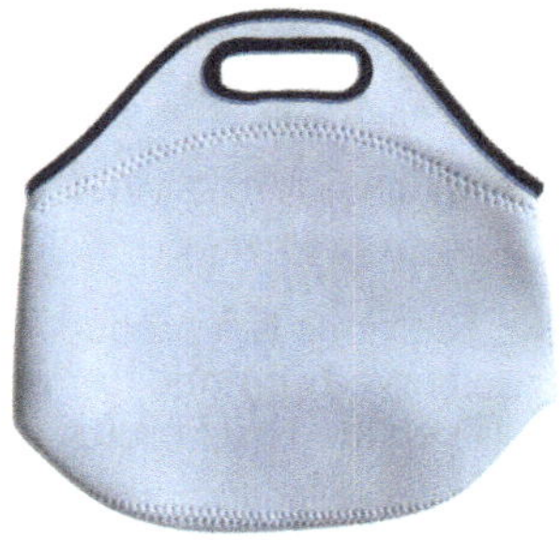

Neoprene is a synthetic rubber material that is often used for insulation of heated or cooled items.

INGREDIENTS

- ☐ Glitter heat transfer vinyl
- ☐ Base material, such as neoprene lunch bag
- ☐ Cover sheets

EQUIPMENT

- ☐ Lint roller
- ☐ Weeding tool
- ☐ Flat heat source such as a heat press
- ☐ (Optional) Heat-resistant tape

PREPARATION

Start with a new neoprene item, such as a lunch bag. **Use a lint roller** if necessary to remove dust and debris.

Pre-heat your flat heat press to the temperature shown in chart below.

Place the vinyl with the glitter side down on the machine mat with the dull side facing up. Then use your cutting machine to **cut your desired pattern out of the vinyl. Weed as necessary** to remove any excess vinyl from the design.

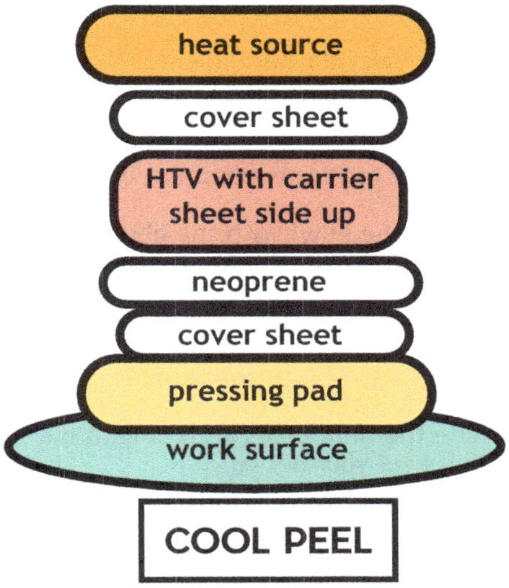
heat source
cover sheet
HTV with carrier sheet side up
neoprene
cover sheet
pressing pad
work surface
COOL PEEL

Place a cover sheet on top of your pressing pad.

Place the neoprene flat, with the seams on the sides, on top of the cover sheet. Place another cover sheet on top of the neoprene and then **pre-press for 5 seconds.**

Remove the top cover sheet.

Place the vinyl on the neoprene with the carrier sheet facing up.

Optionally, use heat-resistant tape to secure the design to the lunch bag.

Place the **cover sheet over the top of the vinyl carrier sheet** to avoid overheating the vinyl or melting the neoprene.

Press according to the chart below.

Once the lunch bag has cooled, **slowly remove the carrier sheet.** If your vinyl peels away from the neoprene, carefully replace carrier sheet and apply a little more heat and pressure.

COOK TIMES

Here are typical times you can use as a starting point. Always check the manufacturer's instructions for time and temperature, when available.

your favorite settings

Traditional Heat Press	AutoPress	EasyPress	Mini Press	
280°F / 138°C	280°F / 138°C	280°F / 138°C	Medium	
20 seconds	15 seconds	20 seconds	20 seconds	
50 psi (Firm pressure)	Auto pressure	Firm pressure	Firm pressure	

TIPS & TRICKS

- × Do not wash your item for at least 24 hours after applying the HTV. If possible, turn item inside out before washing.
- ✓ Remember to mirror your design if it contains words or phrases.

GLITTER HTV

CERAMIC
Mug, mug without handles, pencil cup

Ceramic is a product formed by clay that has been hardened by high heat. This recipe is for curved ceramic items such as mugs. . Mugs with heat transfer vinyl require two heat sources to get the best results.

INGREDIENTS
☐ Glitter heat transfer vinyl
☐ Base material, such as ceramic mug

EQUIPMENT
☐ Rubbing alcohol
☐ Microfiber cloth
☐ Heat-resistant gloves
☐ Heat-resistant tape
☐ Oven-safe tray
☐ Weeding tool
☐ Mini Press
☐ Oven

PREPARATION

Start with a new ceramic item, such as a mug, for the best results.

Pre-heat your mini press and oven to the temperatures shown in the chart below.

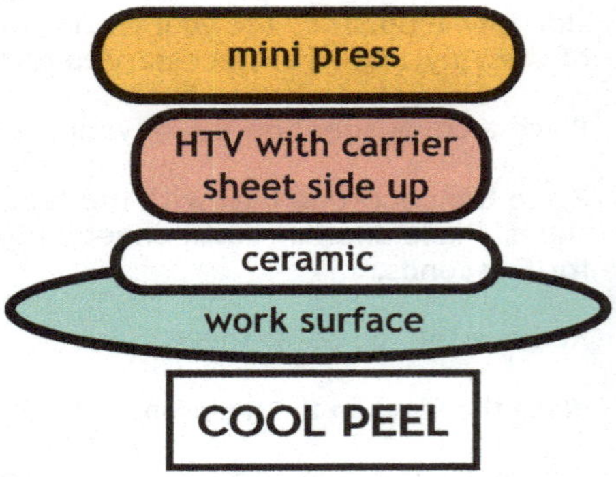

Use the rubbing alcohol and microfiber cloth to gently clean the outside surface of the ceramic. **Let dry completely.**

Place the vinyl with the glitter side down on the machine mat with the dull side facing up. Then use your cutting machine to **cut your desired pattern out of the vinyl. Weed as necessary** to remove any excess vinyl from the design.

Place the vinyl on the ceramic with the carrier sheet facing up.

Use the mini press according to the chart below to press each section or letter of your design.

Let cool, then **slowly peel the carrier sheet away.**

Place the ceramic on an oven-safe tray and place both in your oven according to the chart below.

Once time is up, **use oven mitts to remove the tray and ceramic from the oven.** Let cool completely.

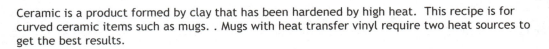

COOL PEEL

COOK TIMES
Here are typical times you can use as a starting point. Always check the manufacturer's instructions for time and temperature, when available.

your favorite settings

Mini Press		Oven	
High	THEN	300°F / 149°C	
30 seconds		15 minutes	
Medium pressure			

TIPS & TRICKS
✓ Mugs with heat transfer vinyl applied are dishwasher safe. Wash in the top rack on normal cycle.
✓ Your household oven is safe to use for this project. You can also use a tabletop convection or toaster oven.

CHAPTER 6
FOIL HTV

FOIL HTV

POLYESTER

Stuffed plushie, backpack, blanket, dress, hoodie, infant bodysuit, long-sleeved shirt, lounge pants, pajamas, pillowcase, polo shirt, shorts, tank top, t-shirt

Polyester is a blend of synthetic materials and is one of the most commonly used materials for textiles. Heat transfer vinyl is easily applied with low heat and medium to firm pressure.

INGREDIENTS
☐ Foil heat transfer vinyl
☐ Base material, such as polyester stuffed plushie
☐ Cover sheet

EQUIPMENT
☐ Weeding tool
☐ Lint roller
☐ Flat heat source such as a heat press
☐ (Optional) Heat-resistant tape

PREPARATION

Start with a new polyester item, such as a stuffed plushie, for the best results. No need to pre-wash, but if you do, avoid fabric softener.

Pre-heat your flat heat press to the temperature listed below.

Place the vinyl with the white carrier sheet side facing down on the machine mat and then use your cutting machine to **cut your desired pattern out of the vinyl. Weed as necessary** to remove any excess vinyl from the design.

Place the polyester item directly on the pressing pad, **with the side you want to apply the HTV facing up.**

Pre-press the polyester item for 10 seconds.

Place the vinyl on the polyester item with the carrier sheet facing up.

Optionally, you can secure the design to the polyester using heat-resistant tape.

Place a cover sheet over the carrier sheet and vinyl.

Press according to the chart below.

Allow to cool. **Slowly peel away your carrier sheet once it is cool to the touch.** If your vinyl peels away from the polyester item, carefully replace carrier sheet and apply a little more heat and pressure.

Stack (top to bottom):
- heat source
- cover sheet
- HTV with carrier sheet side up
- polyester
- pressing pad
- work surface

COOL PEEL

COOK TIMES
Here are typical times you can use as a starting point. Always check the manufacturer's instructions for time and temperature, when available.

Traditional Heat Press	AutoPress	EasyPress	Mini Press	*your favorite settings*
330°F / 166°C	295°F / 146°C	295°F / 146°C	Medium	
30 seconds	30 seconds	30 seconds	25 sec then flip +15 sec	
50 psi (Firm pressure)	Auto pressure	Firm pressure	Firm pressure	

TIPS & TRICKS
✗ Do not wash your item for at least 24 hours after applying the HTV. If you wash a garment, turn it inside out first.
✓ Remember to mirror your design if it contains words or phrases.
✓ You can apply multiple designs to one stuffed plushie. Allow to cool for a few minutes before applying additional HTV to the other areas.

FOIL HTV

COTTON

T-shirt, blanket, burp cloth, denim, dress, hoodie, infant bodysuit, long-sleeved shirt, lounge pants, pajamas, pillowcase, plushie, polo shirt, shorts, sweatshirt, tank top

Items made from 100% cotton work well for heat transfer vinyl. The versatility of the material makes it appropriate for a variety of uses from household items to clothing.

INGREDIENTS
- ☐ Foil heat transfer vinyl
- ☐ Base material, such as 100% cotton t-shirt
- ☐ Cover sheet

EQUIPMENT
- ☐ Lint roller
- ☐ Weeding tool
- ☐ Flat heat source such as a heat press
- ☐ (Optional) T-shirt ruler for placement
- ☐ (Optional) Pressing pillow or foam

PREPARATION

Start with a new 100% cotton item, such as T-shirt. No need to pre-wash, but if you do, avoid fabric softener.

Pre-heat your flat heat press to the temperature shown in chart below.

Place the vinyl with the white carrier sheet side facing down on the machine mat and then use your cutting machine to **cut your desired pattern out of the vinyl. Weed as necessary** to remove any excess vinyl from the design.

Place your cotton material on top of the pressing pad.

Use the lint roller to clean any dust, debris, or loose fibers on the cotton material.

If you're pressing a shirt, fold the shirt in half lengthwise so both sides match up, then **press for 5 seconds** — this both pre-heats the shirt to remove moisture and gives you a straight vertical crease for alignment.

Unfold the cotton material and optionally, **slide a pressing pillow inside to provide support.**

Place the vinyl on the cotton material with the carrier sheet facing up. Place a cover sheet over the carrier sheet.

Press according to the chart below.

Allow to cool to the touch. Then, **slowly peel away your carrier sheet.**

Layer stack (bottom to top): work surface, pressing pad, pillow or foam* , cotton, HTV with carrier sheet side up, cover sheet, heat source.

COOL PEEL

*optional

COOK TIMES
Here are typical times you can use as a starting point. Always check the manufacturer's instructions for time and temperature, when available.

Traditional Heat Press	AutoPress	EasyPress	Mini Press	your favorite settings
290°F / 143°C	290°F / 143°C	295°F / 146°C	Low	
30 seconds	40 seconds	30 seconds	25 sec then flip +15 sec	
50 psi (Firm pressure)	Auto pressure	Firm pressure	Firm pressure	

TIPS & TRICKS
- ✓ Remember to mirror your design if it contains words or phrases.
- ✗ Do not wash your item for at least 24 hours after applying the HTV. If you wash a garment, turn it inside out first.

COTTON/POLY BLEND

Pajamas, blanket, burp cloth, dress, hoodie, infant bodysuit, long-sleeved shirt, lounge pants, pillowcase, plushie, polo shirt, shorts, sweatshirt, tank top, t-shirt

Cotton blends, often found as 50/50 cotton/polyester, of any color are a popular base material for foil heat transfer vinyl. The vinyl can be applied almost anywhere on the material.

INGREDIENTS

- ☐ Foil heat transfer vinyl
- ☐ Base material, such as cotton blend pajamas
- ☐ Cover sheet

EQUIPMENT

- ☐ Lint roller
- ☐ Weeding tool
- ☐ Flat heat source such as a heat press
- ☐ (Optional) Pressing pillow or foam

PREPARATION

Start with a new cotton/polyester blend item, such as a pajama set, for the best results. No need to pre-wash, but if you do, avoid fabric softener.

Pre-heat your flat heat press to the temperature shown in chart below.

Place the vinyl with the white carrier sheet side facing down on the machine mat and then use your cutting machine to **cut your desired pattern out of the vinyl. Weed as necessary** to remove any excess vinyl from the design.

Place the area of the cotton/poly blend material that you plan to apply the vinyl to on top of the pressing pad.

Use the lint roller to clean any dust, debris, or loose fibers on the cotton/poly blend material.

If you're pressing a shirt, fold the shirt in half lengthwise so both sides match up, then **press for 5 seconds** – this both pre-heats the shirt to remove moisture and gives you a straight vertical crease for alignment.

Unfold the cotton/poly blend material. Optionally, slide a pressing pillow inside to provide additional support.

Place the vinyl on the cotton/poly blend material with the carrier sheet facing up.

Place a cover sheet over the carrier sheet to avoid overheating the vinyl.

Press according to the chart below.

Allow to cool to the touch, then **slowly peel away your carrier sheet.**

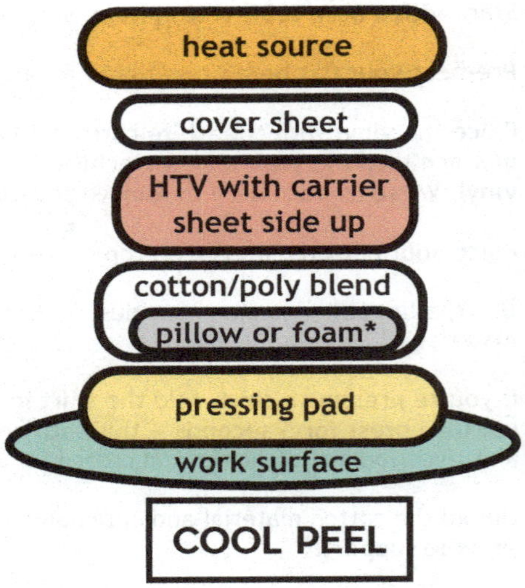
heat source
cover sheet
HTV with carrier sheet side up
cotton/poly blend
pillow or foam*
pressing pad
work surface
COOL PEEL

*optional

COOK TIMES

Here are typical times you can use as a starting point. Always check the manufacturer's instructions for time and temperature, when available.

your favorite settings

Traditional Heat Press	AutoPress	EasyPress	Mini Press	
295°F / 146°C	295°F / 146°C	295°F / 146°C	Low	
40 seconds	40 seconds	30 seconds	25 seconds then flip +15 sec	
50 psi (Firm pressure)	Auto pressure	Firm pressure	Firm pressure	

TIPS & TRICKS

✓ Remember to mirror your design if it contains words or phrases.

FOIL HTV

CANVAS

Placemat, art canvas, backdrop, cooler, flag, reverse art canvas, sail, shoes, tent, tote bag

Make sure your canvas is made of polyester or cotton and does not have any plastic components, which can melt. Plain canvas is usually cream to tan, but can be dyed any color. Canvas fabric can be very smooth or more roughly textured.

INGREDIENTS
☐ Foil heat transfer vinyl
☐ Base material, such as canvas placemat
☐ Cover sheet

EQUIPMENT
☐ Lint roller
☐ Weeding tool
☐ Flat heat source such as a heat press
☐ (Optional) ruler for placement help

PREPARATION

Start with a new canvas item, such as a blank canvas placemat.

Pre-heat your flat heat press to the temperature shown in chart below.

Place the vinyl with the white carrier sheet side facing down on the machine mat and then use your cutting machine to **cut your desired pattern out of the vinyl. Weed as necessary** to remove any excess vinyl from the design.

Place your canvas on top of the pressing pad. **Pre-press for 5 seconds.**

Place the vinyl on the canvas with the carrier sheet facing up.

Cover the carrier sheet with a cover sheet to help avoid overheating the vinyl.

Press according to the chart below.

Once you have applied the appropriate amount of heat and pressure, allow to cool to the touch. Then, **slowly peel away your carrier sheet.**

If your vinyl peels away from the canvas, carefully replace carrier sheet and apply a little more heat and pressure.

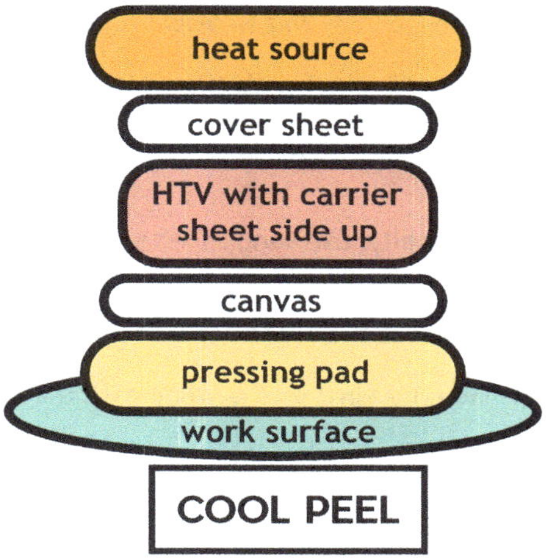

Stack (top to bottom):
- heat source
- cover sheet
- HTV with carrier sheet side up
- canvas
- pressing pad
- work surface

COOL PEEL

COOK TIMES

Here are typical times you can use as a starting point. Always check the manufacturer's instructions for time and temperature, when available.

your favorite settings

Traditional Heat Press	AutoPress	EasyPress	Mini Press	
290°F / 143°C	290°F / 143°C	290°F / 143°C	Low	
20 seconds	20 seconds	20 seconds	25 seconds	
50 psi (Firm pressure)	Auto pressure	Firm pressure	Firm pressure	

TIPS & TRICKS

✗ Do not wash your item for at least 24 hours after applying the HTV. If possible, turn item inside out before washing.
✓ Remember to mirror your design if it contains words or phrases.

FOIL HTV

WOOD

Yard sign, door sign, crate, cutting board, doorknob hanger, sign, charcuterie board

Wood comes in a variety of finishes and can be painted or stained. Wood can be used both as flat panels and in the construction of 3D objects, such as crates.

INGREDIENTS
☐ Foil heat transfer vinyl
☐ Base material, such as wood yard sign
☐ Cover sheet
☐ (Optional) Sandpaper

EQUIPMENT
☐ Microfiber cloth
☐ Weeding tool
☐ Flat heat source such as a heat press
☐ (Optional) Ruler for placement help

PREPARATION

Start with a new wood item, such as a wood sign, for the best results.

Pre-heat your flat heat press to the temperature shown in chart below.

Place the vinyl with the white carrier sheet side facing down on the machine mat and then use your cutting machine to **cut your desired pattern out of the vinyl. Weed as necessary** to remove any excess vinyl from the design.

Optionally, use sandpaper to smooth out the wood surface. Use a microfiber cloth to clean the face of the wood

Pre-press the wood for 5 seconds to eliminate any moisture.

Place the vinyl on the wood with the carrier sheet facing up.

Optionally, you can use a ruler for placement help.

Cover the carrier sheet and vinyl with a cover sheet to help avoid overheating the vinyl.

Press according to the chart below.

Allow to cool to the touch. Then, **slowly peel away your carrier sheet.** If your vinyl peels away from the wood, carefully replace carrier sheet and apply a little more heat and pressure.

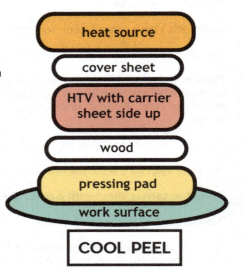

COOK TIMES
Here are typical times you can use as a starting point. Always check the manufacturer's instructions for time and temperature, when available.

your favorite settings

Traditional Heat Press	AutoPress	EasyPress	Mini Press	
305°F / 152°C	305°F / 152°C	305°F / 152°C	Medium	
30 seconds	30 seconds	30 seconds	30 seconds	
50 psi (Firm pressure)	Auto pressure	Firm pressure	Firm pressure	

TIPS & TRICKS
✓ Remember to mirror your design if it contains words or phrases.
✓ You can use varnish, stain, or paint before applying vinyl. Let dry completely before applying vinyl.
✓ For a HTV applied to wood sign tutorial check out jennifermaker.com/htv-on-wood-signs
✗ If applying to a wood cutting board keep in mind that HTV is not food safe.

FOIL HTV

CORK
Trivet, coaster, corkboard, serving tray, yoga block

Cork is a natural material that is lightweight and water-resistant. It can be flexible or made to be stiff and is usually used in home decor and accessories.

INGREDIENTS
☐ Foil heat transfer vinyl
☐ Base material, such as cork trivet
☐ Cover sheet

EQUIPMENT
☐ Lint roller
☐ Weeding tool
☐ Flat heat source such as a heat press
☐ (Optional) Ruler for placement help

PREPARATION

Start with a new cork item, such as a trivet, for the best results.

Pre-heat your flat heat press to the temperature shown in chart below.

Place the vinyl with the white carrier sheet side facing down on the machine mat and then use your cutting machine to **cut your desired pattern out of the vinyl. Weed as necessary** to remove any excess vinyl from the design.

Use a **lint roller to remove** any dust or fibers from the cork

Pre-press the cork for 5 seconds to remove any moisture.

Place the vinyl on the cork with the carrier sheet facing up.

Cover the carrier sheet and vinyl with a cover sheet to help avoid overheating the vinyl.

Press according to the chart below.

Let cool, then **slowly peel away the carrier sheet**. If the vinyl peels away from the cork, carefully replace the carrier sheet and apply a little more heat and pressure for a short amount of time.

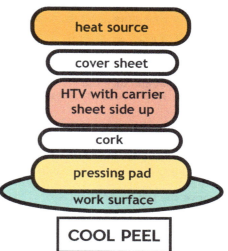

COOK TIMES
Here are typical times you can use as a starting point. Always check the manufacturer's instructions for time and temperature, when available.

Traditional Heat Press	AutoPress	EasyPress	Mini Press	*your favorite settings*
315°F / 157°C	315°F / 157°C	315°F / 157°C	Medium	
15 seconds	15 seconds	15 seconds	25 seconds	
50 psi (Firm pressure)	Auto pressure	Firm pressure	Firm pressure	

TIPS & TRICKS
✗ Use caution when placing heated items on the trivet after application of HTV.
✓ Remember to mirror your design if it contains words or phrases.
✓ Check out a tutorial on customized cork coasters here jennifermaker.com/custom-cork-coasters/

FOIL HTV

NEOPRENE

Chapstick holder, coaster, drink sleeve, flip flops, kneeling pad, laptop sleeve, lunch bag, mousepad, sanitizer bottle holder

Neoprene is a synthetic rubber material that is often used for insulation of heated or cooled items.

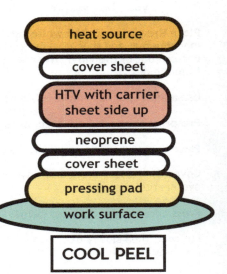

INGREDIENTS
- ☐ Foil heat transfer vinyl
- ☐ Base material, such as neoprene chapstick holder
- ☐ Cover sheets

EQUIPMENT
- ☐ Lint roller
- ☐ Weeding tool
- ☐ Flat heat source such as a heat press
- ☐ (Optional) Heat-resistant tape

PREPARATION

Start with a new neoprene item, such as a chapstick holder. Use a **lint roller** if necessary to remove dust and debris.

Pre-heat your flat heat press to the temperature shown in chart below.

Place the vinyl with the white carrier sheet side facing down on the machine mat and then use your cutting machine to **cut your desired pattern out of the vinyl. Weed as necessary** to remove any excess vinyl from the design.

Place a cover sheet on top of your pressing pad.

Place the neoprene on top of the cover sheet. Place another cover sheet on top of the neoprene and then **pre-press for 5 seconds.**

Remove the top cover sheet.

Place the vinyl on the neoprene with the carrier sheet facing up.

Optionally, use heat-resistant tape to secure the vinyl to the neoprene.

Place the cover sheet over the top of the vinyl carrier sheet to avoid overheating the vinyl or melting the neoprene.

Press according to the chart below.

Once the item has cooled, slowly remove the carrier sheet. If your vinyl peels away from the neoprene, carefully replace carrier sheet and apply a little more heat and pressure.

Stack (top to bottom): heat source, cover sheet, HTV with carrier sheet side up, neoprene, cover sheet, pressing pad, work surface. **COOL PEEL**

COOK TIMES

Here are typical times you can use as a starting point. Always check the manufacturer's instructions for time and temperature, when available.

your favorite settings

Traditional Heat Press	AutoPress	EasyPress	Mini Press	
280°F / 138°C	280°F / 138°C	280°F / 138°C	Medium	
20 seconds	15 seconds	20 seconds	20 seconds	
50 psi (Firm pressure)	Auto pressure	Firm pressure	Firm pressure	

TIPS & TRICKS

- ✓ Remember to mirror your design if it contains words or phrases.
- ✓ Wait until the chapstick holder has cooled completely before inserting a tube of chapstick.
- ✗ Do not wash your item for at least 24 hours after applying the HTV. If possible, turn item inside out before washing.

CHAPTER 7
PATTERNED HTV

PATTERNED HTV

COTTON

Polo shirt, blanket, burp cloth, denim, dress, hoodie, infant bodysuit, long-sleeved shirt, lounge pants, pajamas, pillowcase, plushie, shorts, sweatshirt, tank top, t-shirt

Items made from 100% cotton work well for heat transfer vinyl. The versatility of the material makes it appropriate for a variety of uses from household items to clothing. Check to see whether your patterned vinyl requires mirroring or not, as manufacturers differ.

INGREDIENTS
- ☐ Patterned heat transfer vinyl
- ☐ Base material, such as cotton polo shirt
- ☐ Cover sheet

EQUIPMENT
- ☐ Lint roller
- ☐ Weeding tool
- ☐ Flat heat source such as a heat press
- ☐ (Optional) T-shirt ruler for placement help
- ☐ (Optional) Pillow or foam insert

PREPARATION

Start with a new cotton item, such as a polo shirt. No need to pre-wash, but if you do, avoid fabric softener.

Pre-heat your flat heat press to the temperature shown in chart below.

Place the vinyl with the carrier sheet side facing down on a machine mat and then use your cutting machine to **cut your desired pattern out of the vinyl. Weed as necessary** to remove any excess vinyl from the design.

Use a **lint roller** to remove any dust or fibers from the cotton material.

If you're pressing a shirt, fold the shirt in half lengthwise so both sides match up, then **press for 5 seconds** — this both pre-heats the shirt to remove moisture and gives you a straight vertical crease for alignment.

Unfold the cotton material and lay it flat. Optionally, slide a pressing pillow inside the cotton material to provide additional support.

Place the vinyl on the cotton material with the carrier sheet facing up.

Cover the carrier sheet and vinyl with a cover sheet to help avoid overheating the vinyl.

Press according to the chart below.

Let cool, then slowly peel away the carrier sheet.

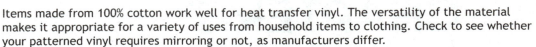

Stack (top to bottom): heat source / cover sheet / HTV with carrier sheet side up / cotton / pillow or foam* / pressing pad / work surface

COOL PEEL

optional

COOK TIMES

Here are typical times you can use as a starting point. Always check the manufacturer's instructions for time and temperature, when available.

Traditional Heat Press	AutoPress	EasyPress	Mini Press	your favorite settings
340°F / 171°C	340°F / 171°C	340°F / 171°C	Medium	
30 seconds	30 seconds	30 seconds	25 sec then flip +15 sec	
50 psi (Firm pressure)	Auto pressure	Firm pressure	Firm pressure	

TIPS & TRICKS

- ✓ Vinyl can also be applied to the sleeves or even the collar of a polo shirt.
- ✗ Do not wash for at least 24 hours after applying vinyl.

PATTERNED HTV

POLYESTER

T-shirt, backpack, blanket, dress, hoodie, infant bodysuit, long-sleeved shirt, lounge pants, pajamas, pillowcase, plushie, polo shirt, shorts, tank top

Polyester is a blend of synthetic materials and is one of the most commonly used materials for textiles. Heat transfer vinyl is easily applied with low heat and medium to firm pressure. Check to see whether your patterned vinyl requires mirroring or not, as manufacturers differ.

INGREDIENTS
- ☐ Patterned heat transfer vinyl
- ☐ Base material, such as polyester T-shirt
- ☐ Cover sheet

EQUIPMENT
- ☐ Lint roller
- ☐ Weeding tool
- ☐ Flat heat source such as a heat press
- ☐ (Optional) T-shirt ruler for placement help
- ☐ (Optional) Pillow or foam insert

PREPARATION

Start with a new polyester item, such as a T-shirt. No need to pre-wash, but if you do, avoid fabric softener.

Pre-heat your flat heat press to the temperature shown in chart below.

Place the vinyl with the carrier sheet side facing down on a machine mat and then use your cutting machine to **cut your desired pattern out of the vinyl. Weed as necessary** to remove any excess vinyl from the design.

Use a lint roller to remove any dust or fibers from the polyester material.

If you're pressing a shirt, fold the shirt in half lengthwise so both sides match up, then **press for 5 seconds** — this both pre-heats the shirt to remove moisture and gives you a straight vertical crease for alignment.

Unfold the polyester material and lay it flat. Optionally, slide a pressing pillow inside the shirt to provide additional support.

Place the vinyl on the polyester material with the carrier sheet facing up.

Cover the carrier sheet and vinyl with a cover sheet in order to help avoid overheating the vinyl.

Press according to the chart below.

Let cool, then slowly peel away the carrier sheet.

Stack (top to bottom):
- heat source
- cover sheet
- HTV with carrier sheet side up
- polyester
- pillow or foam*
- pressing pad
- work surface

COOL PEEL

optional

COOK TIMES
Here are typical times you can use as a starting point. Always check the manufacturer's instructions for time and temperature, when available.

your favorite settings

Traditional Heat Press	AutoPress	EasyPress	Mini Press	
330°F / 166°C	330°F / 166°C	330°F / 166°C	Medium	
30 seconds	30 seconds	30 seconds	25 sec then flip + 15 sec	
50 psi (Firm pressure)	Auto pressure	Firm pressure	Firm pressure	

TIPS & TRICKS
✗ Do not wash your item for at least 24 hours after applying the HTV. If you wash a garment, turn it inside out first.

PATTERNED HTV

WOOD

Door knob hanger, door sign, crate, cutting board, sign, yard sign, charcuterie board

Wood comes in a variety of finishes and can be painted or stained. Wood can be used both as flat panels and in the construction of 3D objects, such as crates. Check to see whether your patterned vinyl requires mirroring or not, as manufacturers differ.

INGREDIENTS
☐ Patterned heat transfer vinyl
☐ Base material, such as wood door knob hanger
☐ Cover sheet
☐ (Optional) Sandpaper

EQUIPMENT
☐ Microfiber cloth
☐ Weeding tool
☐ Flat heat source such as a heat press
☐ (Optional) Ruler for placement help
☐ (Optional) Heat-resistant tape

PREPARATION

Start with a new wood item, such as a door knob hanger.

Pre-heat your flat heat press to the temperature shown in chart below.

Place the vinyl with the carrier sheet side facing down on a machine mat and then use your cutting machine to **cut your desired pattern out of the vinyl**. **Weed as necessary** to remove any excess vinyl from the design.

If desired, **lightly sand the surface of the wood. Use a microfiber cloth** to clean the surface of the wood.

Place a cover sheet over the wood and **pre-press for 5 seconds**.

Place the vinyl on the wood with the carrier sheet facing up.

Optionally, secure the design to the wood using heat-resistant tape.

Cover the carrier sheet and vinyl with a cover sheet in order to help avoid overheating the vinyl.

Press according to the chart below.

Let cool, then slowly peel away the carrier sheet. If the vinyl peels away from the wood, carefully replace the carrier sheet and apply a little more heat and pressure for a short amount of time.

If applying vinyl to both sides, allow the first side to cool completely before doing the second side.

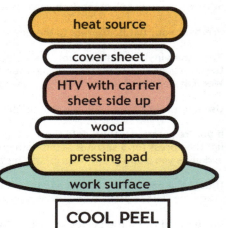

COOK TIMES
Here are typical times you can use as a starting point. Always check the manufacturer's instructions for time and temperature, when available.

your favorite settings

Traditional Heat Press	AutoPress	EasyPress	Mini Press	
305°F / 152°C	305°F / 152°C	305°F / 152°C	Medium	
30 seconds	30 seconds	30 seconds	30 seconds	
50 psi (Firm pressure)	Auto pressure	Firm pressure	Firm pressure	

TIPS & TRICKS
✓ To clean, use a microfiber cloth to gently wipe away dust.
✓ If areas of heat transfer vinyl lift after washing, simply follow the complete application instructions to reapply.

PATTERNED HTV

COTTON/POLY BLEND

Infant bodysuit, blanket, burp cloth, dress, hoodie, long-sleeved shirt, lounge pants, pajamas, pillowcase, plushie, polo shirt, shorts, sweatshirt, tank top, t-shirt

Cotton blends, often found as 50/50 cotton/polyester, of any color are a popular base material for patterned heat transfer vinyl. The vinyl can be applied anywhere on the item. Check to see whether your patterned vinyl requires mirroring or not, as manufacturers differ.

INGREDIENTS
☐ Patterned heat transfer vinyl
☐ Base material, such as cotton blend infant bodysuit
☐ Cover sheet

EQUIPMENT
☐ Lint roller
☐ Weeding tool
☐ Flat heat source such as a heat press
☐ (Optional) T-shirt ruler for placement help
☐ (Optional) Pillow or foam insert

PREPARATION

Start with a new cotton/polyester blend item, such as an infant bodysuit. No need to pre-wash, but if you do, avoid fabric softener.

Pre-heat your flat heat press to the temperature shown in chart below.

Place the vinyl with the carrier sheet side facing down on a machine mat and then use your cutting machine to **cut your desired pattern out of the vinyl. Weed as necessary** to remove any excess vinyl from the design.

Use a lint roller to remove any dust or fibers from the cotton/poly blend material.

If you're pressing a shirt, fold the shirt in half lengthwise so both sides match up, then **press for 5 seconds** — this both pre-heats the shirt to remove moisture and gives you a straight vertical crease for alignment..

Unfold the cotton/poly blend material **and lay it flat.** Optionally, slide a pressing pillow inside the cotton/poly blend material to provide additional support.

Place the vinyl on the cotton/poly blend material **with the carrier sheet facing up. Cover the carrier sheet and vinyl with a cover sheet** to help avoid overheating the vinyl.

Press according to the chart below.

Let cool, then slowly peel away the carrier sheet.

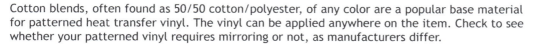

heat source
cover sheet
HTV with carrier sheet side up
cotton/poly blend
pillow or foam*
pressing pad
work surface

COOL PEEL

* optional

COOK TIMES
Here are typical times you can use as a starting point. Always check the manufacturer's instructions for time and temperature, when available.

your favorite settings

Traditional Heat Press	AutoPress	EasyPress	Mini Press	
340°F / 171°C	340°F / 171°C	340°F / 171°C	Medium	
30 seconds	30 seconds	30 seconds	25 sec then flip +15 sec	
50 psi (Firm pressure)	Auto pressure	Firm pressure	Firm pressure	

TIPS & TRICKS
✗ Do not wash your item for at least 24 hours after applying the HTV. If you wash a garment, turn it inside out first.
✓ Remember to mirror your design if it contains words or phrases.

PATTERNED HTV

CANVAS

Placemat, art canvas, backdrop, cooler, flag, reverse art canvas, sail, shoes, tent, tote bag

Make sure your canvas is made of polyester or cotton and does not have any plastic components, which can melt. Plain canvas is usually cream to tan, but can be dyed any color. Canvas fabric can be very smooth or more roughly textured. Check to see whether your patterned vinyl requires mirroring or not, as manufacturers differ.

INGREDIENTS
- ☐ Patterned heat transfer vinyl
- ☐ Base material, such as canvas placemat
- ☐ Cover sheet

EQUIPMENT
- ☐ Lint roller
- ☐ Weeding tool
- ☐ Flat heat source such as a heat press
- ☐ (Optional) Ruler for placement help

PREPARATION

Start with a new canvas item, such as a placemat, for the best results. No need to pre-wash, but if you do, avoid fabric softener.

Pre-heat your flat heat press to the temperature shown in chart below.

Place the vinyl with the carrier sheet side facing down on a machine mat and then use your cutting machine to **cut your desired pattern out of the vinyl. Weed as necessary** to remove any excess vinyl from the design.

Use a lint roller to remove any dust or fibers from the canvas.

Pre-press the canvas for 10 seconds, which will eliminate moisture as well as any wrinkles.

Place the vinyl on the canvas with the carrier sheet facing up.

Cover the carrier sheet and vinyl with a cover sheet to help avoid overheating the vinyl.

Press according to the chart below.

Stack (top to bottom): heat source, cover sheet, HTV with carrier sheet side up, canvas, pressing pad, work surface

COOL PEEL

Let cool, then slowly peel away the carrier sheet. If the vinyl peels away from the canvas, carefully replace the carrier sheet and apply a little more heat and pressure for a short amount of time.

COOK TIMES
Here are typical times you can use as a starting point. Always check the manufacturer's instructions for time and temperature, when available.

your favorite settings

Traditional Heat Press	AutoPress	EasyPress	Mini Press	
340°F / 171°C	340°F / 171°C	340°F / 171°C	Medium	
20 seconds	15 seconds	30 seconds	35 seconds	
50 psi (Firm pressure)	Auto pressure	Firm pressure	Firm pressure	

TIPS & TRICKS
- ✓ Remember to mirror your design if it contains words or phrases.
- ✓ If areas of heat transfer vinyl lift after washing, simply follow the complete application instructions to reapply.
- ✗ Do not wash your item for at least 24 hours after applying the HTV. If possible, turn item inside out before washing.

PATTERNED HTV

FAUX LEATHER

Bookmark, baggage tag, cosmetic bag, earrings, journal cover, notebook, tote bag, wallet

Faux leather is a synthetic plastic-based material used to mimic the look of real leather. It is available in a variety of colors and patterns and is often used for accessories rather than apparel. Check to see whether your patterned vinyl requires mirroring or not, as manufacturers differ.

INGREDIENTS
☐ Patterned heat transfer vinyl
☐ Base material, such as faux leather bookmark
☐ Cover sheet

EQUIPMENT
☐ Microfiber cloth
☐ Weeding tool
☐ Flat heat source such as a heat press
☐ (Optional) Ruler for placement help

PREPARATION

Start with a new faux leather item, such as a bookmark, for the best results.

Pre-heat your flat heat press to the temperature shown in chart below.

Place the vinyl with the carrier sheet side facing down on a machine mat and then use your cutting machine to cut your desired pattern out of the vinyl. Weed as necessary to remove any excess vinyl from the design.

Use a microfiber cloth to remove any dust or fibers from the surface of the faux leather.

Place a cover sheet over the faux leather and pre-press for 5 seconds.

Place the vinyl on the faux leather with the carrier sheet facing up.

Optionally, cover the carrier sheet and vinyl with a cover sheet to help avoid overheating the vinyl and melting the faux leather.

Press according to the chart below.

Let cool, then slowly peel away the carrier sheet. If the vinyl peels away from the faux leather, carefully replace the carrier sheet and apply a little more heat and pressure for a short amount of time.

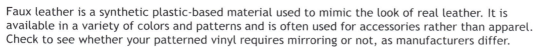

Stack (top to bottom): heat source / cover sheet / HTV with carrier sheet side up / faux leather / pressing pad / work surface

COOL PEEL

COOK TIMES
Here are typical times you can use as a starting point. Always check the manufacturer's instructions for time and temperature, when available.

your favorite settings

Traditional Heat Press	AutoPress	EasyPress	Mini Press	
265°F / 129°C	265°F / 129°C	265°F / 129°C	Low	
15 seconds	15 seconds	20 seconds	30 seconds	
50 psi (Firm pressure)	Auto pressure	Firm pressure	Firm pressure	

TIPS & TRICKS
✗ Do not raise the pressing temperature. This risks melting the faux leather.
✓ If areas of heat transfer vinyl lift after use, simply follow the complete application instructions to reapply.
✓ Remember to mirror your design if it contains words or phrases.

PATTERNED HTV

NEOPRENE

Lunch bag, chapstick holder, coaster, drink sleeve, flip flops, kneeling pad, laptop sleeve, mousepad, sanitizer bottle holder

Neoprene is a synthetic rubber material that is often used for insulation of heated or cooled items. Check to see whether your patterned vinyl requires mirroring or not, as manufacturers differ.

INGREDIENTS
☐ Patterned heat transfer vinyl
☐ Base material, such as neoprene lunch bag
☐ Cover sheets

EQUIPMENT
☐ Lint roller
☐ Weeding tool
☐ Flat heat source such as a heat press
☐ (Optional) Ruler for placement help
☐ (Optional) Pillow or foam insert
☐ (Optional) Heat-resistant tape

PREPARATION

Start with a new neoprene item, such as a lunch bag, for the best results.

Pre-heat your flat heat press to the temperature shown in chart below.

Place the vinyl with the carrier sheet side facing down on a machine mat and then use your cutting machine to **cut your desired pattern out of the vinyl. Weed as necessary** to remove any excess vinyl from the design.

Use a lint roller to remove any dust or fibers from the neoprene.

Place a cover sheet on the pressing pad, then place the neoprene flat on top. **Cover with a cover sheet. Pre-press for 5 seconds, then remove the cover sheet.** Optionally, slide a pressing pillow inside the neoprene to provide additional support.

Place the neoprene on the lunch bag with the carrier sheet facing up.

Optionally, use heat-resistant tape to secure the design to the lunch bag.

Cover the carrier sheet and vinyl with a cover sheet to help avoid overheating the vinyl or the neoprene.

Press according to the chart below.

Let cool, then slowly peel away the carrier sheet.

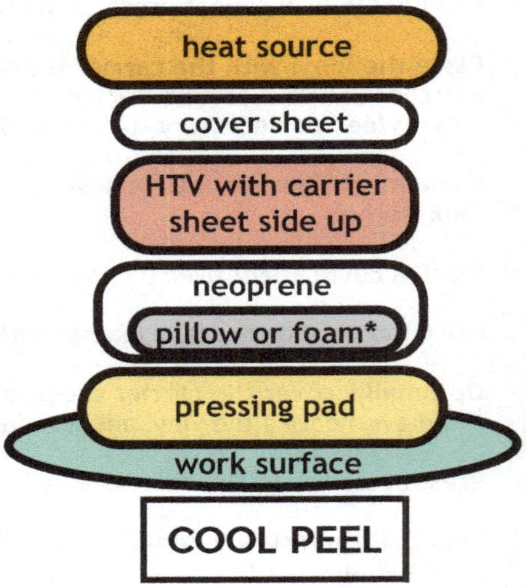

Stack (top to bottom):
- heat source
- cover sheet
- HTV with carrier sheet side up
- neoprene
- pillow or foam*
- pressing pad
- work surface

COOL PEEL

* optional

COOK TIMES
Here are typical times you can use as a starting point. Always check the manufacturer's instructions for time and temperature, when available.

Traditional Heat Press	AutoPress	EasyPress	Mini Press	your favorite settings
280°F / 138°C	280°F / 138°C	280°F / 138°C	Medium	
15 seconds	15 seconds	20 seconds	20 seconds	
50 psi (Firm pressure)	Auto pressure	Firm pressure	Firm pressure	

TIPS & TRICKS
✓ Remember to mirror your design if it contains words or phrases.
✓ If placing vinyl on both sides of the lunch bag, wait until the first side has cooled completely.
✗ Do not wash your item for at least 24 hours after applying the HTV. If possible, turn item inside out before washing.

PATTERNED HTV

CORK

Coasters, corkboard, serving tray, trivet, yoga block

Cork is a natural material that is lightweight and water-resistant. It can be flexible or made to be stiff and is usually used in home decor and accessories. Check to see whether your patterned vinyl requires mirroring or not, as manufacturers differ.

INGREDIENTS
☐ Patterned heat transfer vinyl
☐ Base material, such as cork coasters
☐ Cover sheet

EQUIPMENT
☐ Lint roller
☐ Weeding tool
☐ Flat heat source such as a heat press
☐ (Optional) Ruler for placement help

PREPARATION

Start with a new cork item, such as a coaster, for the best results.

Pre-heat your flat heat press to the temperature shown in chart below.

Place the vinyl with the carrier sheet side facing down on a machine mat and then use your cutting machine to **cut your desired pattern out of the vinyl. Weed as necessary** to remove any excess vinyl from the design.

Use a lint roller to remove any dust or fibers from the cork.

Pre-press your cork for 5 seconds to eliminate moisture.

Place the vinyl on the cork with the carrier sheet facing up.

Cover the carrier sheet and vinyl with a cover sheet to help avoid overheating the vinyl.

Press according to the chart below.

Let cool, then slowly peel away the carrier sheet. If the vinyl peels away from the cork, carefully replace the carrier sheet and apply a little more heat and pressure for a short amount of time.

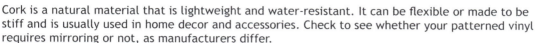

heat source
cover sheet
HTV with carrier sheet side up
cork
pressing pad
work surface

COOL PEEL

COOK TIMES
Here are typical times you can use as a starting point. Always check the manufacturer's instructions for time and temperature, when available.

your favorite settings

Traditional Heat Press	AutoPress	EasyPress	Mini Press	
315°F / 157°C	315°F / 157°C	315°F / 157°C	Medium	
15 seconds	15 seconds	15 seconds	25 seconds	
50 psi (Firm pressure)	Auto pressure	Firm pressure	Firm pressure	

TIPS & TRICKS
✓ To clean, wipe with a microfiber cloth.
✓ If areas of heat transfer vinyl lift after use, simply follow the complete application instructions to reapply.
✓ Remember to mirror your design if it contains words or phrases.
✓ Check out a tutorial on customized cork coasters here jennifermaker.com/custom-cork-coasters/

PATTERNED HTV

CHAMELEON HTV

T-Shirt, athletic wear, blanket, burp cloth, dress, hoodie, infant bodysuit, long-sleeved shirt, lounge pants, pajamas, pillowcase, plushie, polo shirt, shorts, sweatshirt, tank top

HTVront's Chameleon HTV isn't actually patterned, but it does have a color gradient, starting with one color and turning into a second color across each sheet. It can be used on athletic mesh, cotton, polyester, and cotton/polyester blends.

INGREDIENTS
- ☐ Chameleon heat transfer vinyl
- ☐ Base material, such as T-shirt
- ☐ Cover sheet

EQUIPMENT
- ☐ Lint roller
- ☐ Weeding tool
- ☐ Flat heat source such as a heat press
- ☐ (Optional) Ruler for placement help

PREPARATION

Start with a new garment, such as a T-shirt. No need to pre-wash, but if you do, avoid fabric softener. **Use a lint roller** to remove any dust or fibers from the T-shirt.

Pre-heat your flat heat press to the temperature shown in chart below.

Place the vinyl with the carrier sheet side facing down on a machine mat and then use your cutting machine to **cut your desired pattern out of the vinyl. Weed as necessary** to remove any excess vinyl from the design.

If you're pressing a shirt, fold the shirt in half lengthwise so both sides match up, then **press for 5 seconds** — this both pre-heats the shirt to remove moisture and gives you a straight vertical crease for alignment.

Unfold the T-shirt and lay it flat.

Place the vinyl on the T-shirt with the carrier sheet facing up.

Cover the carrier sheet and vinyl with a cover sheet to help avoid overheating the vinyl.

Press according to the chart below.

Let cool completely, then slowly peel away the carrier sheet. If the vinyl peels away from the T-shirt, carefully replace the carrier sheet and apply a little more heat and pressure for a short amount of time.

Layer diagram (top to bottom): heat source, cover sheet, HTV with carrier sheet side up, T-shirt, pressing pad, work surface. **COOL PEEL**

COOK TIMES

Here are typical times you can use as a starting point. Always check the manufacturer's instructions for time and temperature, when available.

your favorite settings

Traditional Heat Press	AutoPress	EasyPress	Mini Press	
315°F / 157°C	315°F / 157°C	315°F / 157°C	Medium	
15 seconds	15 seconds	15 seconds	20 seconds	
40 psi (Medium pressure)	Auto pressure	Medium pressure	Medium pressure	

TIPS & TRICKS
- ✓ If using a home iron, use firm pressure.

CHAPTER 8
GLOW-IN-THE DARK HTV

GLOW-IN-THE-DARK HTV

POLYESTER

Pillowcase, backpack, blanket, dress, hoodie, infant bodysuit, long-sleeved shirt, lounge pants, pajamas, plushie, polo shirt, shorts, tank top, t-shirt

Polyester is a blend of synthetic materials and is one of the most commonly used materials for textiles. Heat transfer vinyl is easily applied with low heat and medium to firm pressure.

INGREDIENTS
- ☐ Glow-in-the-dark heat transfer vinyl
- ☐ Base material, such as polyester pillowcase
- ☐ Cover sheet

EQUIPMENT
- ☐ Weeding tool
- ☐ Lint roller
- ☐ Flat heat source such as a heat press
- ☐ (Optional) Pressing pillow or foam

PREPARATION

Start with a new polyester item, such as a pillowcase, for the best results. No need to pre-wash, but if you do, avoid fabric softener.

Pre-heat your flat heat press to the temperature listed below.

Place the vinyl with the shiny carrier sheet side facing down on a machine mat and then use your cutting machine to **cut your desired pattern out of the vinyl. Weed as necessary** to remove any excess vinyl from the design.

Place the polyester material directly on the pressing pad, with the side you want to apply the vinyl **facing up.**

Optionally, insert a pressing pillow or foam inside of the polyester material for more support.

Cover the polyester material with a cover sheet and **pre-press for 5 seconds** to remove moisture and wrinkles.

Place the vinyl on the polyester material with the carrier sheet facing up.

Place a cover sheet over the carrier sheet.

Press according to the chart below.

Allow to cool. You can **slowly peel away your carrier sheet once it is cool to the touch.** If your vinyl peels away from the polyester material, carefully replace carrier sheet and apply a little more heat and pressure.

Stack (top to bottom): heat source / cover sheet / HTV with carrier sheet side up / polyester / pillow or foam* / pressing pad / work surface

COOL PEEL

*optional

COOK TIMES
Here are typical times you can use as a starting point. Always check the manufacturer's instructions for time and temperature, when available.

your favorite settings

Traditional Heat Press	AutoPress	EasyPress	Mini Press	
305°F / 152°C	305°F / 152°C	305°F / 152°C	Medium	
40 seconds	40 seconds	30 seconds	30 seconds	
50 psi (Firm pressure)	Auto pressure	Firm pressure	Firm pressure	

TIPS & TRICKS
✗ Do not wash your item for at least 24 hours after applying the HTV. If you wash a garment, turn it inside out first.
✓ Glow-in-the-dark vinyl will glow after exposure to direct light.

GLOW-IN-THE-DARK HTV

COTTON

T-shirt, blanket, burp cloth, denim, dress, hoodie, infant bodysuit, long-sleeved shirt, lounge pants, pajamas, pillowcase, plushie, polo shirt, shorts, sweatshirt, tank top

Items made from 100% cotton work well for heat transfer vinyl. The versatility of the material makes it appropriate for a variety of uses from household items to clothing.

INGREDIENTS
☐ Glow-in-the-dark heat transfer vinyl
☐ Base material, such as 100% cotton t-shirt
☐ Cover sheet

EQUIPMENT
☐ Lint roller
☐ Weeding tool
☐ Flat heat source such as a heat press
☐ (Optional) Pressing pillow or foam
☐ (Optional) T-shirt ruler for placement

PREPARATION

Start with a new cotton item, such as a T-shirt. No need to pre-wash, but if you do, avoid fabric softener.

Pre-heat your flat heat press to the temperature shown in chart below.

Place the vinyl with the shiny carrier sheet side facing down on a machine mat and then use your cutting machine to **cut your desired pattern out of the vinyl. Weed as necessary** to remove any excess vinyl from the design.

Place your cotton material on top of the pressing pad.

Use the lint roller to clean any dust or loose fibers on the cotton material.

If you're pressing a shirt, fold the shirt in half lengthwise so both sides match up, then **press for 5 seconds** — this both pre-heats the shirt to remove moisture and gives you a straight vertical crease for alignment.

Unfold the cotton material. Optionally, slide a pressing pillow inside to provide additional support.

Place the vinyl on the cotton material with the carrier sheet facing up.

Place a cover sheet over the carrier sheet.

Press according to the chart below.

Allow to cool to the touch. Then, **slowly peel away your carrier sheet.**

Layer diagram (top to bottom): heat source, cover sheet, HTV with carrier sheet side up, cotton, pillow or foam*, pressing pad, work surface. **COOL PEEL** *optional

COOK TIMES
Here are typical times you can use as a starting point. Always check the manufacturer's instructions for time and temperature, when available.

your favorite settings

Traditional Heat Press	AutoPress	EasyPress	Mini Press	
305°F / 152°C	305°F / 152°C	305°F / 152°C	Medium	
30 seconds	40 seconds	30 seconds	30 seconds	
50 psi (Firm pressure)	Auto pressure	Firm pressure	Firm pressure	

TIPS & TRICKS
✗ Do not wash your item for at least 24 hours after applying the HTV. If you wash a garment, turn it inside out first.
✓ Glow-in-the-dark vinyl will glow after exposure to direct light.

GLOW-IN-THE-DARK HTV

COTTON/POLY BLEND

Long-sleeved shirt, blanket, burp cloth, dress, hoodie, infant bodysuit, lounge pants, pajamas, pillowcase, plushie, polo shirt, shorts, sweatshirt, tank top, t-shirt

Cotton blends, often found as 50/50 cotton/polyester, of any color are a popular base material for glow-in-the-dark heat transfer vinyl. The vinyl can be applied anywhere on the shirt.

INGREDIENTS
☐ Glow-in-the-dark heat transfer vinyl
☐ Base material, such as cotton blend long-sleeved shirt
☐ Cover sheet

EQUIPMENT
☐ Lint roller
☐ Weeding tool
☐ Flat heat source such as a heat press
☐ Pressing pillow or foam

PREPARATION

Start with a new cotton/polyester blend item, such as a long-sleeved shirt. No need to pre-wash, but if you do, avoid fabric softener.

Pre-heat your flat heat press to the temperature shown in chart below.

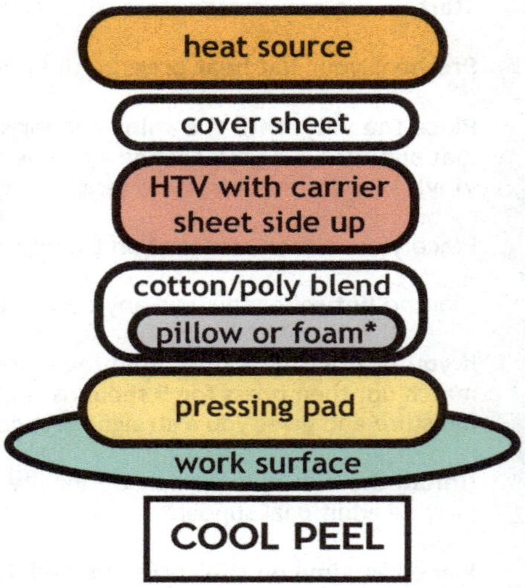

Place the vinyl with the shiny carrier sheet side facing down on a machine mat and then use your cutting machine to **cut your desired pattern out of the vinyl. Weed as necessary** to remove any excess vinyl from the design.

Place the area of the cotton/poly blend material that you plan to apply the vinyl to on top of the pressing pad.

Use the lint roller to clean any dust or loose fibers from the cotton/poly blend material.

If you're pressing a shirt, fold the shirt in half lengthwise so both sides match up, then **press for 5 seconds** — this both pre-heats the shirt to remove moisture and gives you a straight vertical crease for alignment.

Unfold the cotton/poly blend material. Optionally, slide a pressing pillow or foam inside to provide additional support.

Place the vinyl on the cotton/poly blend material with the carrier sheet facing up.

Place a cover sheet over the carrier sheet to avoid overheating the vinyl.

Press according to the chart below.

Let cool to the touch, then **slowly peel away your carrier sheet.**

Layers (top to bottom):
- heat source
- cover sheet
- HTV with carrier sheet side up
- cotton/poly blend
- pillow or foam*
- pressing pad
- work surface

COOL PEEL

*optional

COOK TIMES
Here are typical times you can use as a starting point. Always check the manufacturer's instructions for time and temperature, when available.

Traditional Heat Press	AutoPress	EasyPress	Mini Press	your favorite settings
305°F / 152°C	305°F / 152°C	305°F / 152°C	Medium	
40 seconds	40 seconds	30 seconds	30 seconds	
50 psi (Firm pressure)	Auto pressure	Firm pressure	Firm pressure	

TIPS & TRICKS
× Do not wash your item for at least 24 hours after applying the HTV. If you wash a garment, turn it inside out first.

GLOW-IN-THE-DARK HTV

POLY/NYLON BLEND

Doormat, backpack, dress, infant bodysuit, long-sleeved shirt, pants, polo shirt, shorts, tank top, t-shirt, tote bag

Polyester/nylon blend fabric is made of synthetic material. It is more durable than polyester alone and softer than nylon alone.

INGREDIENTS
- ☐ Glow-in-the-dark heat transfer vinyl
- ☐ Base material, such as polyester-blend doormat
- ☐ Cover sheet

EQUIPMENT
- ☐ Lint roller
- ☐ Flat heat source such as a heat press
- ☐ Weeding tool
- ☐ (Optional) Ruler for placement help
- ☐ (Optional) Heat-resistant tape

PREPARATION

Start with a new polyester/nylon blend item, such as a blank doormat.

Pre-heat your flat heat press to the temperature shown in chart below.

Place the vinyl with the shiny carrier sheet side facing down on a machine mat and then use your cutting machine to **cut your desired pattern out of the vinyl. Weed as necessary** to remove any excess vinyl from the design.

Place your poly/nylon blend material on top of the pressing pad. **Pre-press for 5 seconds.**

Place the vinyl on the poly/nylon blend material with the carrier sheet facing up. Optionally, you can secure the design to the doormat using heat-resistant tape.

Cover the carrier sheet with a cover sheet to help avoid overheating the vinyl.

Press according to the chart below.

Once you have applied the appropriate amount of heat and pressure, allow your item to cool before you **slowly peel away your carrier sheet**.

If your vinyl peels away from the poly/nylon blend material, carefully replace carrier sheet and apply a little more heat and pressure.

COOK TIMES
Here are typical times you can use as a starting point. Always check the manufacturer's instructions for time and temperature, when available.

your favorite settings

Traditional Heat Press	AutoPress	EasyPress	Mini Press	
305°F / 152°C	305°F / 152°C	305°F / 152°C	Medium	
30 seconds	40 seconds	30 seconds	30 seconds	
50 psi (Firm pressure)	Auto pressure	Firm pressure	Firm pressure	

TIPS & TRICKS
- ✗ Do not wash your item for at least 24 hours after applying the HTV. If you wash a garment, turn it inside out first.
- ✓ If your vinyl begins to peel away after repeated use of the doormat, simply re-heat following the directions above.
- ✓ Glow-in-the-dark vinyl will glow after exposure to direct light.

GLOW-IN-THE-DARK HTV

WOOD

Door knob hanger, door sign, crate, cutting board, sign, yard sign, charcuterie board

Wood comes in a variety of finishes and can be painted or stained. Wood can be used both as flat panels and in the construction of 3D objects, such as crates.

INGREDIENTS
- ☐ Glow-in-the-dark heat transfer vinyl
- ☐ Base material, such as wood door knob hanger
- ☐ Cover sheet
- ☐ (Optional) Sandpaper

EQUIPMENT
- ☐ Microfiber cloth
- ☐ Weeding tool
- ☐ Flat heat source such as a heat press
- ☐ (Optional) Ruler for placement help
- ☐ (Optional) Heat-resistant tape

PREPARATION

Start with a new wood item, such as a wood door hanger.

Pre-heat your flat heat press to the temperature shown in chart below.

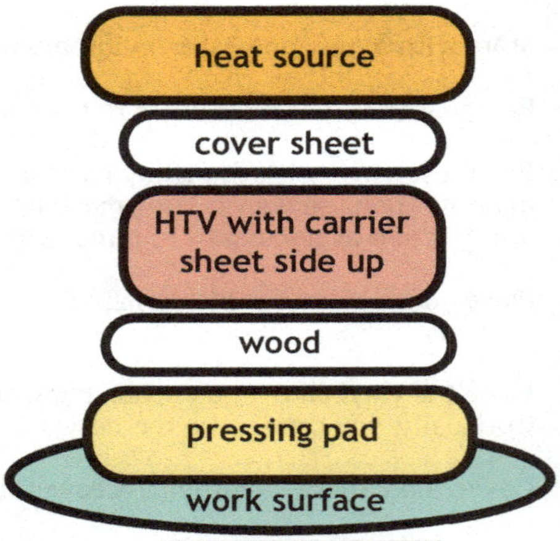

Place the vinyl with the shiny carrier sheet side facing down on a machine mat and then use your cutting machine to **cut your desired pattern out of the vinyl. Weed as necessary** to remove any excess vinyl from the design.

Optionally, use sandpaper to smooth out the wood surface. Use a microfiber cloth to clean the face of your wood.

Pre-press the wood for 5 seconds to eliminate any moisture.

Place the vinyl on the wood with the carrier sheet facing up. Optionally, you can secure the design to the wood using heat-resistant tape.

Optionally, you can use a ruler to help with the vinyl placement.

Cover the carrier sheet and vinyl with a cover sheet to help avoid overheating the vinyl.

Press according to the chart below.

Once you have applied the appropriate amount of heat and pressure, you can **slowly peel away your carrier sheet once it is cool to the touch.** If your vinyl peels away from the wood, carefully replace carrier sheet and apply a little more heat and pressure.

Layers (top to bottom):
- heat source
- cover sheet
- HTV with carrier sheet side up
- wood
- pressing pad
- work surface

COOL PEEL

COOK TIMES

Here are typical times you can use as a starting point. Always check the manufacturer's instructions for time and temperature, when available.

your favorite settings

Traditional Heat Press	AutoPress	EasyPress	Mini Press	
305°F / 152°C	305°F / 152°C	305°F / 152°C	Medium	
45 seconds	45 seconds	30 seconds	40 seconds	
50 psi (Firm pressure)	Auto pressure	Firm pressure	Firm pressure	

TIPS & TRICKS
- ✓ Remember to mirror your design if it contains words or phrases.
- ✓ Glow-in-the-dark vinyl will glow after exposure to direct light.

GLOW-IN-THE-DARK HTV

NEOPRENE

Mousepad, chapstick holder, coaster, drink sleeve, flip flops, kneeling pad, laptop sleeve, lunch bag, sanitizer bottle holder

Neoprene is a synthetic rubber material that is often used for insulation of heated or cooled items.

INGREDIENTS
- ☐ Glow-in-the-dark heat transfer vinyl
- ☐ Base material, such as neoprene mousepad
- ☐ Cover sheets

EQUIPMENT
- ☐ Lint roller
- ☐ Weeding tool
- ☐ Flat heat source such as a heat press
- ☐ (Optional) Heat-resistant tape

PREPARATION

Start with a new neoprene item, such as a mousepad. Use a **lint roller** if necessary to remove dust and debris.

Pre-heat your flat heat press to the temperature shown in chart below.

Place the vinyl with the shiny carrier sheet side facing down on a machine mat and then use your cutting machine to **cut your desired pattern out of the vinyl**. **Weed as necessary** to remove any excess vinyl from the design.

Place a cover sheet on top of your pressing pad.

Place the neoprene on top of the cover sheet. Place another cover sheet on top of the neoprene and then **pre-press for 5 seconds.**

Remove the top cover sheet.

Place the vinyl on the neoprene with the carrier sheet facing up. Optionally, you can secure the design to the neoprene using heat-resistant tape.

Place the **cover sheet over the top of the vinyl carrier sheet** to avoid overheating the vinyl or melting the neoprene

Press according to the chart below.

Once the mousepad has cooled, slowly remove the carrier sheet. If your vinyl peels away from the neoprene, carefully replace carrier sheet and apply a little more heat and pressure.

Stack (top to bottom): heat source / cover sheet / HTV with carrier sheet side up / neoprene / cover sheet / pressing pad / work surface — **COOL PEEL**

COOK TIMES
Here are typical times you can use as a starting point. Always check the manufacturer's instructions for time and temperature, when available.

your favorite settings

Traditional Heat Press	AutoPress	EasyPress	Mini Press	
315°F / 157°C	315°F / 157°C	315°F / 157°C	Medium	
40 seconds	40 seconds	40 seconds	50 seconds	
50 psi (Firm pressure)	Auto pressure	Firm pressure	Firm pressure	

TIPS & TRICKS
- ✓ Remember to mirror your design if it contains words or phrases.
- ✓ Glow-in-the-dark vinyl will glow after direct exposure to light.
- ✗ Do not wash your item for at least 24 hours after applying the HTV. If possible, turn item inside out before washing.

CHAPTER 9
UV COLOR CHANGE HTV

UV COLOR CHANGE HTV

COTTON

Shorts, blanket, burp cloth, denim, dress, hoodie, infant bodysuit, long-sleeved shirt, lounge pants, pajamas, pillowcase, plushie, polo shirt, sweatshirt, tank top, t-shirt

Items made from 100% cotton work well for heat transfer vinyl. The versatility of the material makes it appropriate for a variety of uses from household items to clothing.

INGREDIENTS
☐ UV color change heat transfer vinyl
☐ Base material, such as cotton shorts
☐ Cover sheet

EQUIPMENT
☐ Lint roller
☐ Weeding tool
☐ Flat heat source such as a heat press
☐ (Optional) Ruler for placement help
☐ (Optional) Pillow or foam insert

PREPARATION

Start with a new cotton item, such as pair of shorts, for the best results. No need to pre-wash, but if you do, avoid fabric softener.

Pre-heat your flat heat press to the temperature shown in chart below.

Place the vinyl with the shiny carrier sheet side facing down on a machine mat and then use your cutting machine to **cut your desired pattern out of the vinyl. Weed as necessary** to remove any excess vinyl from the design.

Use a lint roller to remove any dust or fibers from the cotton material.

Pre-press the cotton material for 10 seconds to eliminate moisture and any wrinkles.

Optionally, slide a pressing pillow inside the cotton material to provide additional support.

Place the vinyl on the cotton material with the carrier sheet facing up. Cover the carrier sheet and vinyl with a cover sheet to help avoid overheating the vinyl.

Press according to the chart below.

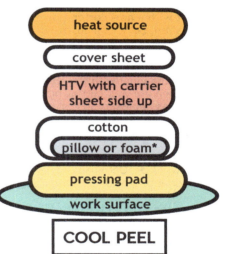

*optional

Let cool, then slowly peel away the carrier sheet. If the vinyl peels away from the cotton material, carefully replace the carrier sheet and apply a little more heat and pressure for a short amount of time.

COOK TIMES
Here are typical times you can use as a starting point. Always check the manufacturer's instructions for time and temperature, when available.

your favorite settings

Traditional Heat Press	AutoPress	EasyPress	Mini Press	
315°F / 157°C	315°F / 157°C	315°F / 157°C	Medium	
35 seconds	40 seconds	30 seconds	30 seconds	
50 psi (Firm pressure)	Auto pressure	Firm pressure	Firm pressure	

TIPS & TRICKS
✓ UV color change vinyl will change color with exposure to sunlight.
✓ Remember to mirror your design if it contains words or phrases.
✓ Check out a tutorial at jennifermaker.com/color-changing-htv

UV COLOR CHANGE HTV

COTTON/POLY BLEND

Pajama pants, blanket, burp cloth, dress, hoodie, infant bodysuit, long-sleeved shirt, lounge pants, pillowcase, plushie, polo shirt, shorts, sweatshirt, tank top, t-shirt

Cotton blends, often found as 50/50 cotton/polyester, of any color are a popular base material for UV color change heat transfer vinyl. The vinyl can be applied anywhere on the shirt.

INGREDIENTS
☐ UV color change heat transfer vinyl
☐ Base material, such as cotton blend pajama pants
☐ Cover sheet

EQUIPMENT
☐ Lint roller
☐ Weeding tool
☐ Flat heat source such as a heat press
☐ (Optional) Ruler for placement help
☐ (Optional) Pillow or foam insert

PREPARATION

Start with a new cotton/polyester blend item, such as a pair of pajama pants, for the best results. No need to pre-wash, but if you do, avoid fabric softener.

Pre-heat your flat heat press to the temperature shown in chart below.

Place the vinyl with the shiny carrier sheet side facing down on a machine mat and then use your cutting machine to **cut your desired pattern out of the vinyl. Weed as necessary** to remove any excess vinyl from the design.

Use a lint roller to remove any dust or fibers from the cotton/poly blend material.

Pre-press the cotton/poly blend material for 10 seconds to eliminate moisture and wrinkles. Optionally, slide a pressing pillow inside the cotton/poly blend material to provide additional support.

Place the vinyl on the cotton/poly blend material with the carrier sheet facing up. Cover the carrier sheet and vinyl with a **cover sheet** to help avoid overheating the vinyl.

Press according to the chart below.

Let cool, then slowly peel away the carrier sheet. If the vinyl peels away from the cotton/poly blend material, carefully replace the carrier sheet and apply a little more heat and pressure for a short amount of time.

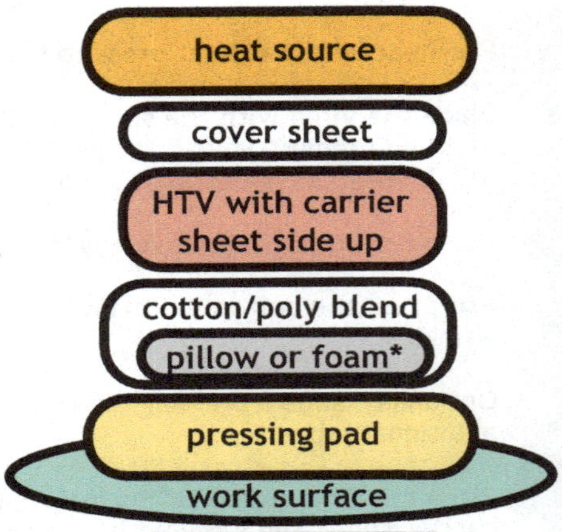

- heat source
- cover sheet
- HTV with carrier sheet side up
- cotton/poly blend
- pillow or foam*
- pressing pad
- work surface

COOL PEEL

* optional

COOK TIMES
Here are typical times you can use as a starting point. Always check the manufacturer's instructions for time and temperature, when available.

your favorite settings

Traditional Heat Press	AutoPress	EasyPress	Mini Press	
315°F / 157°C	315°F / 157°C	315°F / 157°C	Medium	
35 seconds	40 seconds	30 seconds	30 seconds	
50 psi (Firm pressure)	Auto pressure	Firm pressure	Firm pressure	

TIPS & TRICKS
✓ UV color change vinyl will change color with exposure to sunlight.
✓ Remember to mirror your design if it contains words or phrases.
✓ Check out a tutorial at jennifermaker.com/color-changing-htv

UV COLOR CHANGE HTV

POLYESTER

Backpack, blanket, dress, hoodie, infant bodysuit, long-sleeved shirt, lounge pants, pajamas, pillowcase, plushie, polo shirt, shorts, tank top, t-shirt

Polyester is a blend of synthetic materials and is one of the most commonly used materials for textiles. Heat transfer vinyl is easily applied with low heat and medium to firm pressure.

INGREDIENTS
☐ UV color change heat transfer vinyl
☐ Base material, such as polyester backpack
☐ Cover sheet

EQUIPMENT
☐ Lint roller
☐ Weeding tool
☐ Flat heat source such as a heat press
☐ (Optional) Ruler for placement help
☐ (Optional) Pillow or foam insert

PREPARATION

Start with a new polyester item, such as a backpack, for the best results.

Pre-heat your flat heat press to the temperature shown in chart below.

Place the vinyl with the shiny carrier sheet side facing down on a machine mat and then use your cutting machine to **cut your desired pattern out of the vinyl. Weed as necessary** to remove any excess vinyl from the design.

Use a lint roller to remove any dust or fibers from the polyester material.

Place a cover sheet over the polyester material and **pre-press for 10 seconds** to eliminate moisture as well as any wrinkles.

Optionally, slide a pressing pillow inside the polyester material to provide additional support.

Place the vinyl on the polyester material with the carrier sheet facing up.

Cover the carrier sheet and vinyl with a cover sheet to help avoid overheating the vinyl.

Press according to the chart below. Take care to avoid zippers.

Let cool, then slowly peel away the carrier sheet. If the vinyl peels away from the polyester material, carefully replace the carrier sheet and apply a little more heat and pressure for a short amount of time.

Stack (top to bottom): heat source / cover sheet / HTV with carrier sheet side up / polyester / pillow or foam* / pressing pad / work surface

COOL PEEL

* optional

COOK TIMES

Here are typical times you can use as a starting point. Always check the manufacturer's instructions for time and temperature, when available.

your favorite settings

Traditional Heat Press	AutoPress	EasyPress	Mini Press	
315°F / 157°C	315°F / 157°C	315°F / 157°C	Medium	
35 seconds	40 seconds	30 seconds	30 seconds	
50 psi (Firm pressure)	Auto pressure	Firm pressure	Firm pressure	

TIPS & TRICKS
✓ UV color change vinyl will change color with exposure to sunlight.
✓ Remember to mirror your design if it contains words or phrases.
✓ Check out a tutorial at jennifermaker.com/color-changing-htv

UV COLOR CHANGE HTV

CANVAS

Canvas cooler, art canvas, backdrop, flag, reverse art canvas, placemat, sail, shoes, tent, tote bag

Make sure your canvas is made of polyester or cotton and does not have any plastic components, which can melt. Plain canvas is usually cream to tan, but can be dyed any color. Canvas fabric can be very smooth or more roughly textured.

INGREDIENTS
☐ UV color change heat transfer vinyl
☐ Base material, such as canvas cooler
☐ Cover sheet

EQUIPMENT
☐ Lint roller
☐ Weeding tool
☐ Flat heat source such as a heat press
☐ (Optional) Ruler for placement help
☐ (Optional) Pillow or foam insert

PREPARATION

Start with a new canvas item, such as a canvas cooler, for the best results.

Pre-heat your flat heat press to the temperature shown in chart below.

Place the vinyl with the shiny carrier sheet side facing down on a machine mat and then use your cutting machine to **cut your desired pattern out of the vinyl. Weed as necessary** to remove any excess vinyl from the design.

Use a lint roller to remove any dust or fibers from the canvas.

Optionally, slide a pressing pillow inside the canvas to provide additional support and prevent the insulation material from melting together.

Pre-press the side of the canvas that you plan to apply vinyl to for 10 seconds. This will eliminate moisture as well as any wrinkles.

Place the vinyl on the canvas with the carrier sheet facing up.

Cover the carrier sheet and vinyl with a cover sheet to help avoid overheating the vinyl.

Press according to the chart below. Take care to avoid any zippers.

Let cool, then slowly peel away the carrier sheet. If the vinyl peels away from the canvas, carefully replace the carrier sheet and apply a little more heat and pressure for a short amount of time.

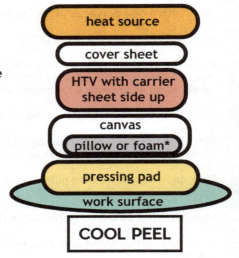

* optional

COOK TIMES
Here are typical times you can use as a starting point. Always check the manufacturer's instructions for time and temperature, when available.

your favorite settings

Traditional Heat Press	AutoPress	EasyPress	Mini Press	
315°F / 157°C	315°F / 157°C	315°F / 157°C	Medium	
35 seconds	40 seconds	30 seconds	30 seconds	
50 psi (Firm pressure)	Auto pressure	Firm pressure	Firm pressure	

TIPS & TRICKS
✓ UV color change vinyl will change color with exposure to sunlight.
✓ Remember to mirror your design if it contains words or phrases.
✗ Do not wash your item for at least 24 hours after applying the HTV. If possible, turn item inside out before washing.

UV COLOR CHANGE HTV

WOOD

Wood sign, door sign, crate, cutting board, doorknob hanger, yard sign, charcuterie board

Wood comes in a variety of finishes and can be painted or stained. Wood can be used both as flat panels and in the construction of 3D objects, such as crates.

INGREDIENTS
☐ UV color change heat transfer vinyl
☐ Base material, such as unfinished wood sign
☐ Cover sheet
☐ (Optional) Sandpaper

EQUIPMENT
☐ Microfiber cloth
☐ Weeding tool
☐ Flat heat source such as a heat press
☐ (Optional) Ruler for placement help
☐ (Optional) Heat-resistant tape
☐ (Optional) Scraper

PREPARATION

Start with a new wood item, such as a wood sign, for the best results.

Pre-heat your flat heat press to the temperature shown in chart below.

Place the vinyl with the shiny carrier sheet side facing down on a machine mat and then use your cutting machine to cut your desired pattern out of the vinyl. Weed as necessary to remove any excess vinyl from the design.

If desired, lightly sand the surface of the wood. Use a microfiber cloth to clean the surface of the wood.

Pre-press the wood for 5 seconds.

Place the vinyl on the wood with the carrier sheet facing up. Optionally, secure the design to the wood using heat-resistant tape.

Optionally, cover the carrier sheet and vinyl with a cover sheet to help avoid overheating the vinyl.

Press according to the chart below.

Let cool, then slowly peel away the carrier sheet. If the vinyl peels away from the wood, carefully replace the carrier sheet and apply a little more heat and pressure for a short amount of time, then use a scraper to push the vinyl down into place.

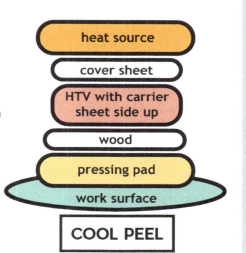

COOK TIMES
Here are typical times you can use as a starting point. Always check the manufacturer's instructions for time and temperature, when available.

your favorite settings

Traditional Heat Press	AutoPress	EasyPress	Mini Press	
315°F / 157°C	315°F / 157°C	315°F / 157°C	Medium	
35 seconds	40 seconds	30 seconds	30 seconds	
50 psi (Firm pressure)	Auto pressure	Firm pressure	Firm pressure	

TIPS & TRICKS
✓ UV color change vinyl will change color with exposure to sunlight.
✓ Remember to mirror your design if it contains words or phrases.
✓ Use paint, stain, or varnish before applying vinyl. Let dry completely prior to vinyl application.
✓ Check out a tutorial at jennifermaker.com/color-changing-htv

UV COLOR CHANGE HTV

NEOPRENE

Drink sleeve, chapstick holder, coaster, flip flops, kneeling pad, laptop sleeve, lunch bag, mousepad, sanitizer bottle holder

Neoprene is a synthetic rubber material that is often used for insulation of heated or cooled items.

INGREDIENTS
- ☐ UV color change heat transfer vinyl
- ☐ Base material, such as neoprene drink sleeve
- ☐ Cover sheets

EQUIPMENT
- ☐ Lint roller
- ☐ Weeding tool
- ☐ Flat heat source such as a heat press
- ☐ (Optional) Ruler for placement help
- ☐ (Optional) Heat-resistant tape

PREPARATION

Start with a new neoprene item, such as a drink sleeve, for the best results.

Pre-heat your flat heat press to the temperature shown in chart below.

Place the vinyl with the shiny carrier sheet side facing down on a machine mat and then use your cutting machine to **cut your desired pattern out of the vinyl. Weed as necessary** to remove any excess vinyl from the design.

Use a lint roller to remove any dust or fibers from the neoprene.

Lay two cover sheets over the neoprene and **pre-press for 10 seconds** to eliminate any moisture. If using a traditional heat press or AutoPress, lay a cover sheet on top of the platen to prevent the neoprene from sticking to the platen. **After pre-pressing, remove the top cover sheets.**

Place the vinyl on the neoprene with the carrier sheet facing up.

Optionally, use heat-resistant tape to secure the design to the neoprene.

Cover the carrier sheet and vinyl with a cover sheet to help avoid overheating the vinyl or burning the neoprene.

Press according to the chart below.

Let cool, then slowly peel away the carrier sheet. If the vinyl peels away from the neoprene, carefully replace the carrier sheet and apply a little more heat and pressure for a short amount of time.

If applying vinyl to both sides of the drink neoprene, let the first side cool completely before doing the second side.

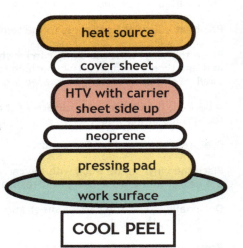

COOL PEEL

COOK TIMES
Here are typical times you can use as a starting point. Always check the manufacturer's instructions for time and temperature, when available.

Traditional Heat Press	AutoPress	EasyPress	Mini Press	your favorite settings
315°F / 157°C	315°F / 157°C	315°F / 157°C	Medium	
35 seconds	40 seconds	30 seconds	30 seconds	
50 psi (firm pressure)	Auto pressure	Firm pressure	Firm pressure	

TIPS & TRICKS
- ✓ UV color change vinyl will change color with exposure to sunlight.
- ✓ Remember to mirror your design.
- ✗ Do not wash your item for at least 24 hours after applying the HTV. If possible, turn item inside out before washing.

UV COLOR CHANGE HTV

BURLAP

Garden flag, bag, banner, bunting, pillowcase, table runner, wine bag, wreath

Burlap is a material made of plant fibers. Natural burlap comes in shades of brown, but it can be dyed any color. Burlap fabric is textured and can be tightly or loosely woven.

INGREDIENTS
- ☐ UV color change heat transfer vinyl
- ☐ Base material, such as burlap garden flag
- ☐ Cover sheet

EQUIPMENT
- ☐ Lint roller
- ☐ Weeding tool
- ☐ Flat heat source such as a heat press
- ☐ (Optional) Ruler for placement help

PREPARATION

Start with a new burlap item, such as a garden flag, for the best results.

Pre-heat your flat heat press to the temperature shown in chart below.

Place the vinyl with the shiny carrier sheet side facing down on a machine mat and then use your cutting machine to **cut your desired pattern out of the vinyl. Weed as necessary** to remove any excess vinyl from the design.

Use a lint roller to remove any dust or loose fibers from the burlap.

Fold the burlap in half lengthwise so both sides match up, then **pre-press for 5 seconds** — this both pre-heats the burlap to remove moisture and gives you a straight vertical crease for alignment.

Unfold the burlap and lay it flat.

Place the vinyl on the burlap with the carrier sheet facing up.

Cover the carrier sheet and vinyl with a cover sheet to help avoid overheating the vinyl.

Press according to the chart below.

Let cool, then slowly peel away the carrier sheet. If the vinyl peels away from the burlap, carefully replace the carrier sheet and apply a little more heat and pressure for a short amount of time.

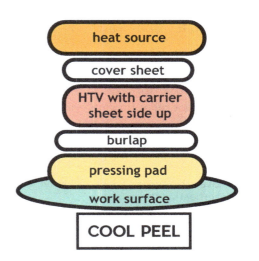

COOK TIMES

Here are typical times you can use as a starting point. Always check the manufacturer's instructions for time and temperature, when available.

your favorite settings

Traditional Heat Press	AutoPress	EasyPress	Mini Press	
315°F / 157°C	315°F / 157°C	315°F / 157°C	Medium	
40 seconds	40 seconds	45 seconds	45 seconds	
50 psi (Firm pressure)	Auto pressure	Firm pressure	Firm pressure	

TIPS & TRICKS
- ✓ UV color change vinyl will change color with exposure to sunlight.
- ✓ Remember to mirror your design.
- ✓ Check out a tutorial at jennifermaker.com/color-changing-htv

UV COLOR CHANGE HTV

CORK
Corkboard, coaster, serving tray, trivet, yoga block

Cork is a natural material that is lightweight and water-resistant. It can be flexible or made to be stiff and is usually used in home decor and accessories.

INGREDIENTS
☐ UV color change heat transfer vinyl
☐ Base material, such as corkboard
☐ Cover sheet

EQUIPMENT
☐ Lint roller
☐ Weeding tool
☐ Flat heat source such as a heat press
☐ (Optional) Ruler for placement help

PREPARATION

Start with a new cork item, such as a corkboard, for the best results.

Pre-heat your flat heat press to the temperature shown in chart below.

Place the vinyl with the shiny carrier sheet side facing down on a machine mat and then use your cutting machine to **cut your desired pattern out of the vinyl. Weed as necessary** to remove any excess vinyl from the design.

Use a lint roller to remove any dust or fibers from the cork.

Pre-press the cork for 5 seconds to remove any moisture.

Place the vinyl on the cork with the carrier sheet facing up.

Cover the carrier sheet and vinyl with a cover sheet to help avoid overheating the vinyl.

Press according to the chart below.

Let cool, then slowly peel away the carrier sheet. If the vinyl peels away from the cork, carefully replace the carrier sheet and apply a little more heat and pressure for a short amount of time.

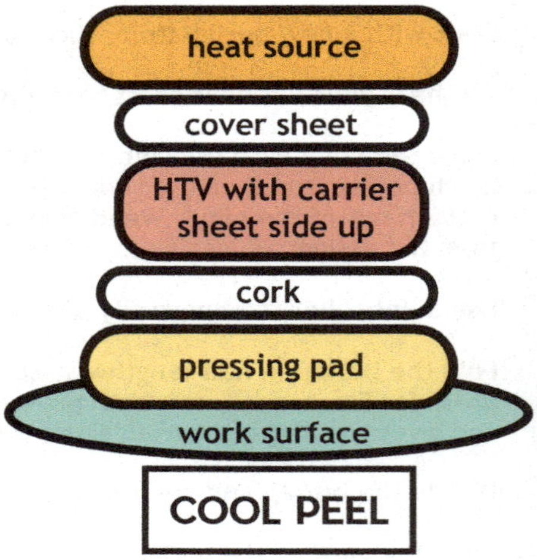

Stack order: heat source / cover sheet / HTV with carrier sheet side up / cork / pressing pad / work surface

COOL PEEL

COOK TIMES
Here are typical times you can use as a starting point. Always check the manufacturer's instructions for time and temperature, when available.

Traditional Heat Press	AutoPress	EasyPress	Mini Press	your favorite settings
315°F / 157°C	315°F / 157°C	315°F / 157°C	Medium	
40 seconds	40 seconds	30 seconds	30 seconds	
50 psi (Firm pressure)	Auto pressure	Firm pressure	Firm pressure	

TIPS & TRICKS
✓ UV color change vinyl will change color with exposure to sunlight.
✓ Remember to mirror your design if it contains words or phrases.
✓ Wait until the corkboard has cooled completely before using tacks and pins.
✓ Check out a tutorial at jennifermaker.com/color-changing-htv

UV COLOR CHANGE HTV

FAUX LEATHER

Bifold wallet, baggage tag, bookmark, cosmetic bag, earrings, journal cover, notebook, tote bag

Faux leather is a synthetic plastic-based material used to mimic the look of real leather. It is available in a variety of colors and patterns and is often used for accessories rather than apparel.

INGREDIENTS
☐ UV color change heat transfer vinyl
☐ Base material, such as faux leather bifold wallet
☐ Cover sheet

EQUIPMENT
☐ Microfiber cloth
☐ Weeding tool
☐ Flat heat source such as a heat press
☐ (Optional) Ruler for placement help

PREPARATION

Start with a new faux leather item, such as a bifold wallet, for the best results.

Pre-heat your flat heat press to the temperature shown in chart below.

Place the vinyl with the shiny carrier sheet side facing down on a machine mat and then use your cutting machine to **cut your desired pattern out of the vinyl. Weed as necessary** to remove any excess vinyl from the design.

Use a microfiber cloth to remove any dust or fibers from the faux leather.

Place a cover sheet on the pressing pad and place the faux leather on top. If possible, lay the faux leather totally flat.

Preheat the faux leather for 5 seconds.

Place the vinyl on the faux leather with the carrier sheet facing up.

Cover the carrier sheet and vinyl with a cover sheet to help avoid overheating the vinyl or melting the faux leather.

Press according to the chart below.

Let cool, then slowly peel away the carrier sheet. If the vinyl peels away from the faux leather, carefully replace the carrier sheet and apply a little more heat and pressure for a short amount of time.

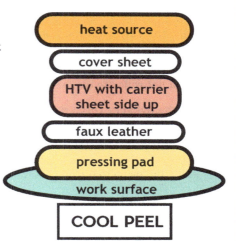

COOK TIMES
Here are typical times you can use as a starting point. Always check the manufacturer's instructions for time and temperature, when available.

your favorite settings

Traditional Heat Press	AutoPress	EasyPress	Mini Press	
315°F / 157°C	315°F / 157°C	315°F / 157°C	Medium	
30 seconds	30 seconds	20 seconds	20 seconds	
Light pressure	Auto pressure	Light pressure	Firm pressure	

TIPS & TRICKS
✓ UV color change vinyl will change color with exposure to sunlight.
✓ Remember to mirror your design if it contains words or phrases.
✓ You can also apply HTV to the inside of the wallet to personalize.
✓ Check out a tutorial at jennifermaker.com/color-changing-htv

UV COLOR CHANGE HTV

NYLON

Drawstring bag, activewear, backpack, poncho, puff vest, swimwear, tech accessory bag, umbrella, windbreaker

Nylon is a synthetic fabric with a variety of uses. It can melt or burn, so extra care is needed when applying heat transfer vinyl.

INGREDIENTS
- ☐ UV color change heat transfer vinyl
- ☐ Base material, such as nylon drawstring bag
- ☐ Cover sheets

EQUIPMENT
- ☐ Lint roller
- ☐ Weeding tool
- ☐ Flat heat source such as a heat press
- ☐ Ruler for placement help
- ☐ (Optional) Pillow or foam insert

PREPARATION

Start with a new nylon item, such as a drawstring bag, for the best results. **Pre-heat your flat heat press** to the temperature shown in chart below.

Place the vinyl with the shiny carrier sheet side facing down on a machine mat and then use your cutting machine to **cut your desired pattern out of the vinyl. Weed as necessary** to remove any excess vinyl from the design.

Use a lint roller to remove any dust or fibers from the nylon.

Lay the nylon material flat, cover with a cover sheet, then **pre-press for 10 seconds** — this both pre-heats the nylon to remove moisture and gives you a straight vertical crease for alignment.

Place a cover sheet on the pressing pad. Optionally, slide a pressing pillow inside the nylon to provide additional support.

Place the vinyl on the nylon with the carrier sheet facing up.

Cover the carrier sheet and vinyl with a cover sheet to help avoid overheating the vinyl or melting the nylon.

Press according to the chart below. Take care to keep the drawstrings out of the pressing area.

Let cool, then slowly peel away the carrier sheet. If the vinyl peels away from the nylon, carefully replace the carrier sheet and apply a little more heat and pressure for a short amount of time.

Stack (top to bottom):
- heat source
- cover sheet
- HTV with carrier sheet side up
- nylon
- pillow or foam*
- pressing pad
- work surface

COOL PEEL

* optional

COOK TIMES

Here are typical times you can use as a starting point. Always check the manufacturer's instructions for time and temperature, when available.

your favorite settings

Traditional Heat Press	AutoPress	EasyPress	Mini Press	
315°F / 157°C	315°F / 157°C	315°F / 157°C	Medium	
35 seconds	40 seconds	30 seconds	30 seconds	
50 psi (Firm pressure)	Auto pressure	Firm pressure	Firm pressure	

TIPS & TRICKS
✓ UV color change vinyl will change color with exposure to sunlight.
✓ Remember to mirror your design if it contains words or phrases.

CHAPTER 10
PUFF HTV

PUFF HTV

COTTON

Denim jacket, blanket, burp cloth, dress, hoodie, infant bodysuit, long-sleeved shirt, lounge pants, pajamas, pillowcase, plushie, polo shirt, shorts, sweatshirt, tank top, t-shirt

Items made from 100% cotton work well for heat transfer vinyl. The versatility of the material makes it appropriate for a variety of uses from household items to clothing.

INGREDIENTS
☐ Puff heat transfer vinyl
☐ Base material, such as 100% cotton denim jacket
☐ Cover sheet

EQUIPMENT
☐ Lint roller
☐ Weeding tool
☐ Flat heat source such as a heat press
☐ Wood cutting board or hard pressing surface
☐ (Optional) T-shirt ruler for placement

PREPARATION

Start with a new 100% cotton item, like a denim jacket, for the best results. No need to pre-wash, but if you do, avoid fabric softener.

Pre-heat your flat heat press to the temperature shown in chart below.

Place the vinyl with the shiny carrier sheet side facing down on a machine mat and then use your cutting machine to **cut your desired pattern out of the vinyl. Weed as necessary** to remove any excess vinyl from the design.

Place your cotton fabric on top of the wood cutting board placed on a sturdy surface. Make sure that you have a sturdy pressing area; puff vinyl needs hard pressure to apply correctly.

Use the lint roller to clean any dust or loose fibers on the cotton fabric.

Pre-press for 30-40 seconds to remove moisture from the material.

Fold the cotton fabric in half lengthwise so both sides match up, then press for 5 seconds — this will give you a straight vertical crease for alignment.

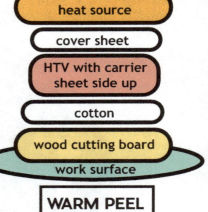

Place the vinyl on the cotton fabric with the carrier sheet facing up. Place a cover sheet over the carrier sheet.

Press according to the chart below.

Quickly peel away your carrier sheet while it is still warm.

COOK TIMES

Here are typical times you can use as a starting point. Always check the manufacturer's instructions for time and temperature, when available.

your favorite settings

Traditional Heat Press	AutoPress	EasyPress	Mini Press	
305°F / 152°C	305°F / 152°C	305°F / 152°C	Medium	
30 seconds	40 seconds	30 seconds	30 seconds	
50 psi (Firm pressure)	Auto pressure	Firm pressure	Firm pressure	

TIPS & TRICKS

✓ If your puff vinyl is not smooth, you can quickly reapply the carrier sheet and apply a little more heat and pressure; however, this can impact the overall outcome of the puff vinyl.
✗ Do not wash your item for at least 24 hours after applying the HTV. If you wash a garment, turn it inside out first.
✓ For a tutorial on puff vinyl, check out jennifermaker.com/how-to-use-puff-vinyl

PUFF HTV

COTTON/POLY BLEND

T-shirt, blanket, burp cloth, dress, hoodie, infant bodysuit, long-sleeved shirt, lounge pants, pajamas, pillowcase, plushie, polo shirt, shorts, sweatshirt, tank top

Cotton blends, often found as 50/50 cotton/polyester, of any color are a popular base material for puff heat transfer vinyl. The vinyl can be applied anywhere on the shirt.

INGREDIENTS
- ☐ Puff heat transfer vinyl
- ☐ Base material, such as cotton blend T-shirt
- ☐ Cover sheet

EQUIPMENT
- ☐ Lint roller
- ☐ Weeding tool
- ☐ Thick wooden cutting board or hard surface to press on
- ☐ Flat heat source such as a heat press
- ☐ (Optional) T-shirt ruler for alignment help

PREPARATION

Start with a new cotton/polyester blend item, such as a T-shirt, for the best results. Pre-washing your shirt is recommended for better puff vinyl application; however, avoid fabric softener.

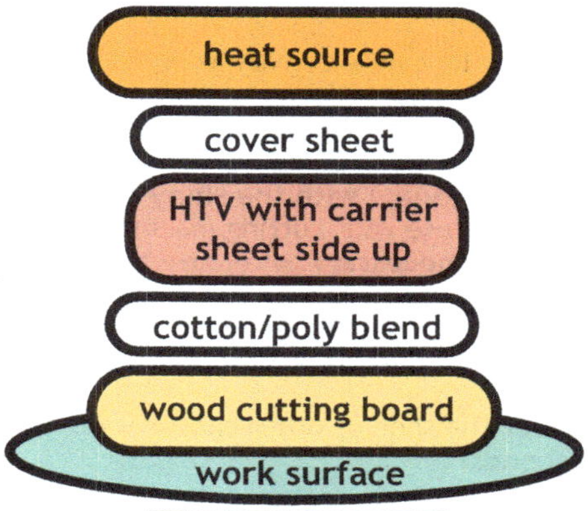

Pre-heat your flat heat press to the temperature shown in chart below.

Place the vinyl with the shiny carrier sheet side facing down on a machine mat and then use your cutting machine to **cut your desired pattern out of the vinyl. Weed as necessary** to remove any excess vinyl from the design.

Place the area of the cotton/poly blend material that you plan to apply the vinyl to on top of wood cutting board or hard pressing surface.

Pre-press your cotton/blend material for 30-40 seconds to remove moisture. Removing additional moisture will help the puff vinyl stay smooth.

Use the lint roller to remove any dust or loose fibers from the cotton/poly blend material.

If you're pressing a shirt, fold the shirt in half lengthwise so both sides match up, then **press for 5 seconds** — this both pre-heats the shirt to remove moisture and gives you a straight vertical crease for alignment.

Place the vinyl on the cotton/poly blend material with the carrier sheet facing up. Place a cover sheet over the carrier sheet.

Make sure that you have a sturdy pressing area because puff vinyl needs hard pressure to apply correctly.

Press according to the chart below.

While still warm, quickly peel away the carrier sheet. If your vinyl texture is not smooth, you can reapply the carrier sheet and apply a little more heat and pressure to smooth it out.

Stack (top to bottom): heat source → cover sheet → HTV with carrier sheet side up → cotton/poly blend → wood cutting board → work surface. **WARM PEEL**

COOK TIMES
Here are typical times you can use as a starting point. Always check the manufacturer's instructions for time and temperature, when available.

your favorite settings

Traditional Heat Press	AutoPress	EasyPress	Mini Press	
280°F / 138°C	280°F / 138°C	305°F / 152°C	Medium	
10 seconds	10 seconds	10 seconds	15 seconds	
50 psi (Firm pressure)	Auto pressure	Firm pressure	Firm pressure	

TIPS & TRICKS
- ✗ Do not wash your item for at least 24 hours after applying the HTV. If you wash a garment, turn it inside out first.
- ✓ If using the AutoPress, use a pressing pad with a 1-inch thick wood cutting board on top, then place your shirt on top to press.

PUFF HTV

CANVAS

Shoes, art canvas, backdrop, cooler, flag, reverse art canvas, placemat, sail, tent, tote bag

Make sure your canvas is made of polyester or cotton and does not have any plastic components, which can melt. Plain canvas is usually cream to tan, but can be dyed any color. Canvas fabric can be very smooth or more roughly textured.

INGREDIENTS
- ☐ Puff heat transfer vinyl
- ☐ Base material, such as canvas shoe(s)
- ☐ Cover sheet

EQUIPMENT
- ☐ Microfiber cloth
- ☐ Weeding tool
- ☐ Flat heat source such as a heat press
- ☐ Rolled sock or washcloth to place inside shoe
- ☐ Heat-resistant tape

PREPARATION

Start with a new canvas item, such as canvas shoes, for the best results.

Pre-heat your flat heat press to the temperature shown in chart below.

Place the vinyl with the shiny carrier sheet side facing down on a machine mat and then use your cutting machine to **cut your desired pattern out of the vinyl. Weed as necessary** to remove any excess vinyl from the design.

If placing vinyl on canvas shoes, roll a washcloth or sock and place inside the shoe.

Cover the shoe or other canvas item with the cover sheet and **pre-press for 5-10 seconds.**

Place the vinyl on the shoe or other canvas item with the carrier sheet facing up.

If making shoes, use heat-resistant tape to secure the **vinyl design** to the shoe.

Place a cover sheet over the canvas item.

Press according to the chart below.

While still warm, quickly peel away the carrier sheet.

Stack (top to bottom): heat source / cover sheet / HTV with carrier sheet side up / rolled sock / canvas shoe / work surface

WARM PEEL

COOK TIMES

Here are typical times you can use as a starting point. Always check the manufacturer's instructions for time and temperature, when available.

your favorite settings

Traditional Heat Press	AutoPress	EasyPress	Mini Press	
305°F / 152°C	305°F / 152°C	305°F / 152°C	Medium	
15 seconds	15 seconds	15 seconds	15 seconds	
50 psi (Firm pressure)	Auto pressure	Firm pressure	Firm pressure	

TIPS & TRICKS

- ✗ Do not wash shoes for at least 24 hours after vinyl application.
- ✓ Don't forget to mirror your design if your design has words or phrases.
- ✗ Do not wash your item for at least 24 hours after applying the HTV. If possible, turn item inside out before washing.
- ✓ For a tutorial on applying HTV to canvas shoes, check out jennifermaker.com/personalize-your-shoes-iron-on-vinyl
- ✓ For a tutorial on puff vinyl, check out jennifermaker.com/how-to-use-puff-vinyl

PUFF HTV

FELT

Bag, basket, bunting, flowers, home decor, lamp shade, mobile, ornament, pillow, placemat, sleep mask, travel organizer

Felt is a very versatile fabric that is often used for accessories and decor. It is available in a wide variety of colors, prints, and thicknesses, as well as pre-stiffened or soft.

INGREDIENTS
☐ Puff heat transfer vinyl
☐ Base material, such as felt bag
☐ Cover sheet

EQUIPMENT
☐ Lint roller
☐ Weeding tool
☐ Wood cutting board or hard flat surface to press on
☐ Flat heat source such as a heat press
☐ (Optional) Ruler for placement help

PREPARATION

Start with a new felt item, such as a bag, for the best results.

Pre-heat your flat heat press to the temperature shown in chart below.

Place the vinyl with the shiny carrier sheet side facing down on a machine mat and then use your cutting machine to **cut your desired pattern out of the vinyl. Weed as necessary** to remove any excess vinyl from the design.

Use a lint roller to remove any dust or debris from the felt.

Place your felt on top of a wood cutting board or hard flat surface to press on. Make sure that you have a sturdy pressing area; puff vinyl needs hard pressure to apply correctly.

Pre-press your felt for 5 seconds to remove any moisture and wrinkles.

Place the vinyl on the felt with the carrier sheet facing up.

Place a cover sheet over the top of the vinyl carrier sheet to avoid overheating the vinyl.

Press according to the chart below.

While still warm, quickly peel away the carrier sheet.

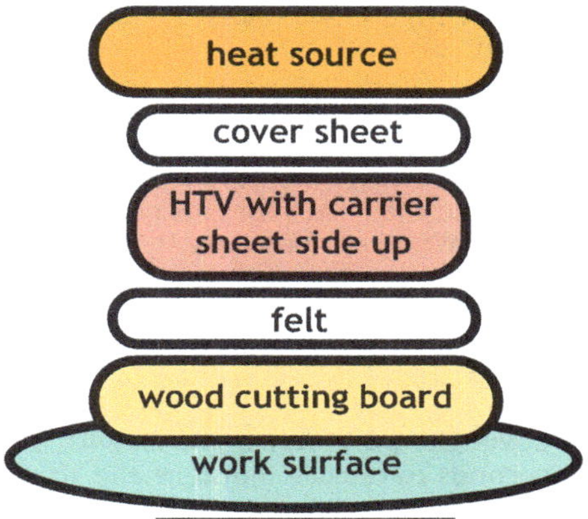

Stack (top to bottom):
- heat source
- cover sheet
- HTV with carrier sheet side up
- felt
- wood cutting board
- work surface

WARM PEEL

COOK TIMES
Here are typical times you can use as a starting point. Always check the manufacturer's instructions for time and temperature, when available.

your favorite settings

Traditional Heat Press	AutoPress	EasyPress	Mini Press	
280°F / 138°C	280°F / 138°C	280°F / 138°C	Medium	
10 seconds	10 seconds	15 seconds	15 seconds	
50 psi (Firm pressure)	Auto pressure	Firm pressure	Firm pressure	

TIPS & TRICKS
✓ The carrier sheet should hold the vinyl in place; however, you can use heat-resistant tape to secure if needed.
✓ If the puff vinyl is not smooth after application, you can quickly repress; however, keep in mind that this can impact the overall quality of the puff vinyl.
✗ Do not wash your item for at least 24 hours after applying the HTV. If possible, turn item inside out before washing.
✓ For a tutorial on puff vinyl, check out jennifermaker.com/how-to-use-puff-vinyl

PUFF HTV

POLYESTER

Shorts, backpack, blanket, dress, hoodie, infant bodysuit, long-sleeved shirt, lounge pants, pajamas, pillowcase, plushie, polo shirt, tank top, t-shirt

Polyester is a blend of synthetic materials and is one of the most commonly used materials for textiles. Heat transfer vinyl is easily applied with low heat and medium to firm pressure.

INGREDIENTS
- ☐ Puff heat transfer vinyl
- ☐ Base material, such as polyester shorts
- ☐ Cover sheet

EQUIPMENT
- ☐ Weeding tool
- ☐ Lint roller
- ☐ Flat heat source such as a heat press
- ☐ Wood cutting board or hard pressing surface

PREPARATION

Start with a new polyester item, such as a pair of shorts, for the best results. No need to pre-wash, but if you do, avoid fabric softener.

Pre-heat your flat heat press to the temperature listed below.

Place the vinyl with the shiny carrier sheet side facing down on a machine mat and then use your cutting machine to **cut your desired pattern out of the vinyl. Weed as necessary** to remove any excess vinyl from the design.

Place the polyester material directly on the wood cutting board. Make sure that you have a sturdy pressing area; puff vinyl needs hard pressure to apply correctly.

Cover the polyester material with a cover sheet and **pre-press for 10-15 seconds** to remove moisture and wrinkles.

Place the vinyl on the polyester material with the carrier sheet facing up.

Place a cover sheet over the carrier sheet.

Press according to the chart below.

While still warm, quickly peel away the carrier sheet.

Stack (top to bottom):
- heat source
- cover sheet
- HTV with carrier sheet side up
- polyester
- wood cutting board
- work surface

WARM PEEL

COOK TIMES

Here are typical times you can use as a starting point. Always check the manufacturer's instructions for time and temperature, when available.

your favorite settings

Traditional Heat Press	AutoPress	EasyPress	Mini Press	
280°F / 138°C	280°F / 138°C	280°F / 138°C	Medium	
10 seconds	10 seconds	15 seconds	15 seconds	
50 psi (Firm pressure)	Auto pressure	Firm pressure	Firm pressure	

TIPS & TRICKS

- ✗ Do not wash your item for at least 24 hours after applying the HTV. If you wash a garment, turn it inside out first.
- ✓ If the puff vinyl is not smooth after application, you can quickly repress; however, keep in mind that this can impact the overall quality of the puff vinyl.
- ✓ For a tutorial on puff vinyl, check out jennifermaker.com/how-to-use-puff-vinyl

CHAPTER 11
FLOCKED HTV

FLOCKED HTV

COTTON

Burp cloth, blanket, denim, dress, hoodie, infant bodysuit, long-sleeved shirt, lounge pants, pajamas, pillowcase, plushie, polo shirt, shorts, sweatshirt, tank top, t-shirt

Items made from 100% cotton work well for heat transfer vinyl. The versatility of the material makes it appropriate for a variety of uses from household items to clothing.

INGREDIENTS
☐ Flocked heat transfer vinyl
☐ Base material, such as 100% cotton burp cloth
☐ Cover sheet

EQUIPMENT
☐ Lint roller
☐ Weeding tool
☐ Flat heat source such as a heat press

PREPARATION

Start with a new 100% cotton item, such as a burp cloth, for the best results. No need to pre-wash, but if you do, avoid fabric softener.

Pre-heat your flat heat press to the temperature shown in chart below.

Place the vinyl with the shiny carrier sheet side facing down on a machine mat and then use your cutting machine to **cut your desired pattern out of the vinyl. Weed as necessary** to remove any excess vinyl from the design.

Place your cotton material on top of the pressing pad.

Use the lint roller to clean any dust or loose fibers on the cotton material.

Pre-press for 5 seconds to remove moisture from the material.

Place the vinyl on the cotton material with the carrier sheet facing up.

Place a cover sheet over the carrier sheet.

Press according to the chart below.

Once you have applied the appropriate amount of heat and pressure, **allow to cool** before you **peel away your carrier sheet.**

Stack (top to bottom): heat source, cover sheet, HTV with carrier sheet side up, cotton, pressing pad, work surface

COOL PEEL

COOK TIMES
Here are typical times you can use as a starting point. Always check the manufacturer's instructions for time and temperature, when available.

your favorite settings

Traditional Heat Press	AutoPress	EasyPress	Mini Press	
305°F / 152°C	305°F / 152°C	305°F / 152°C	Medium	
15 seconds	15 seconds	15 seconds	15 seconds	
50 psi (Firm pressure)	Auto pressure	Firm pressure	Firm pressure	

TIPS & TRICKS
✗ Do not wash your item for at least 24 hours after applying the HTV. If you wash a garment, turn it inside out first.
✓ If your vinyl begins to peel while removing the carrier sheet, simply replace the carrier sheet and reapply heat and pressure for a few more seconds.
✓ Flocked vinyl has a suede type texture and can be layered on top of a variety of heat transfer vinyl products.

FLOCKED HTV

COTTON/POLY BLEND

Dress, blanket, burp cloth, hoodie, infant bodysuit, long-sleeved shirt, lounge pants, pajamas, pillowcase, plushie, polo shirt, shorts, sweatshirt, tank top, t-shirt

Cotton blends, often found as 50/50 cotton/polyester, of any color are a popular base material for flocked heat transfer vinyl. The vinyl can be applied anywhere on the shirt.

INGREDIENTS
☐ Flocked heat transfer vinyl
☐ Base material, such as cotton blend dress
☐ Cover sheet

EQUIPMENT
☐ Lint roller
☐ Weeding tool
☐ Flat heat source such as a heat press
☐ (Optional) T-shirt ruler for alignment help

PREPARATION

Start with a new cotton/polyester blend item, such as a dress, for best results. No need to pre-wash; however, if you do, avoid fabric softener.

Pre-heat your flat heat press to the temperature shown in chart below.

Place the vinyl with the shiny carrier sheet side facing down on a machine mat and then use your cutting machine to **cut your desired pattern out of the vinyl. Weed as necessary** to remove any excess vinyl from the design.

Place the area of the cotton/poly blend material that you plan to apply the vinyl to on top of the pressing pad.

Use the lint roller to remove any dust or loose fibers from the cotton/poly blend material.

Pre-press your cotton/poly blend material for 10 seconds to remove wrinkles and moisture.

Place the vinyl on the cotton/poly blend material with the carrier sheet facing up.

Place a cover sheet over the carrier sheet to prevent overheating of the vinyl or material.

Press according to the chart below.

Once you have applied the appropriate amount of heat and pressure, allow to cool before removing the carrier sheet.

Stack order (top to bottom):
- heat source
- cover sheet
- HTV with carrier sheet side up
- cotton/poly blend
- pressing pad
- work surface

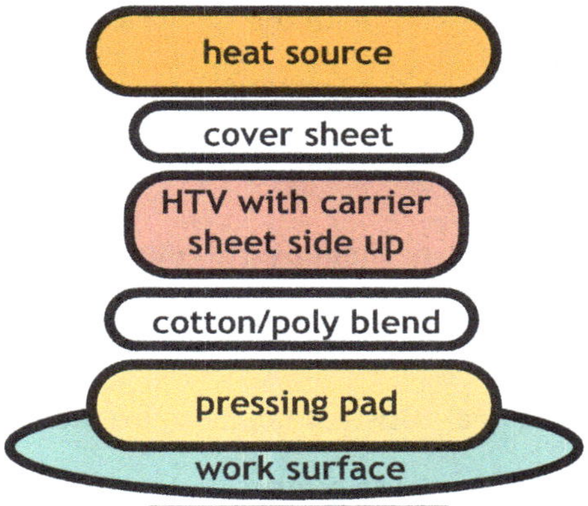

COOL PEEL

COOK TIMES
Here are typical times you can use as a starting point. Always check the manufacturer's instructions for time and temperature, when available.

your favorite settings

Traditional Heat Press	AutoPress	EasyPress	Mini Press	
280°F / 138°C	280°F / 138°C	305°F / 152°C	Medium	
15 seconds	15 seconds	15 seconds	15 seconds	
50 psi (Firm pressure)	Auto pressure	Firm pressure	Firm pressure	

TIPS & TRICKS
✗ Do not wash your item for at least 24 hours after applying the HTV. If you wash a garment, turn it inside out first.
✓ If the vinyl begins to pull away from the fabric as you are removing the carrier sheet, simply replace the carrier sheet and apply a little more heat and pressure.
✓ Flocked vinyl has a suede type texture and can be layered on top of a variety of heat transfer vinyl products.

FLOCKED HTV

SPANDEX

Headband, bike shorts, dress, leggings, leotard, tank top, t-shirt

Spandex is a synthetic fabric that is very stretchy without losing its shape. It is ideal for athletic apparel.

INGREDIENTS
- ☐ Flocked heat transfer vinyl
- ☐ Base material, such as spandex headband
- ☐ Cover sheet

EQUIPMENT
- ☐ Lint roller
- ☐ Weeding tool
- ☐ Flat heat source such as a heat press
- ☐ Heat-resistant tape

PREPARATION

Start with a new spandex item, such as a headband, for the best results.

Pre-heat your flat heat press to the temperature shown in chart below.

Place the vinyl with the shiny carrier sheet side facing down on a machine mat and then use your cutting machine to **cut your desired pattern out of the vinyl. Weed as necessary** to remove any excess vinyl from the design.

Place the spandex on top of the pressing pad. Make sure that the spandex is lying flat.

Place a cover sheet over the spandex and pre-press for 5 seconds.

Place the vinyl on the spandex with the carrier sheet facing up. Do not stretch the spandex.

Using heat-resistant tape, secure the vinyl design to the spandex.

Use the cover to protect the vinyl and spandex.

Press according to the chart below.

Once you have applied the appropriate amount of heat and pressure, allow to cool before removing the carrier sheet.

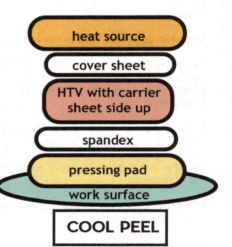

COOL PEEL

COOK TIMES
Here are typical times you can use as a starting point. Always check the manufacturer's instructions for time and temperature, when available.

your favorite settings

Traditional Heat Press	AutoPress	EasyPress	Mini Press	
305°F / 152°C	305°F / 152°C	305°F / 152°C	Medium	
15 seconds	15 seconds	15 seconds	15 seconds	
50 psi (Firm pressure)	Auto pressure	Firm pressure	Firm pressure	

TIPS & TRICKS
- ✗ Do not wash your item for at least 24 hours after applying the HTV. If you wash a garment, turn it inside out first.
- ✓ Don't forget to mirror your design if your design has words or phrases.
- ✓ Flocked vinyl has a suede type texture and can be layered on top of a variety of heat transfer vinyl products.

FLOCKED HTV

FELT

Bag, basket, bunting, flowers, home decor, lamp shade, mobile, ornament, pillow, placemat, sleep mask, travel organizer

Felt is a very versatile fabric that is often used for accessories and decor. It is available in a wide variety of colors, prints, and thicknesses, as well as pre-stiffened or soft.

INGREDIENTS
☐ Flocked heat transfer vinyl
☐ Base material, such as felt bag
☐ Cover sheet

EQUIPMENT
☐ Lint roller
☐ Weeding tool
☐ Flat heat source such as a heat press
☐ (Optional) Ruler for placement help

PREPARATION

Start with a new felt item, such as a bag, for the best results.

Pre-heat your flat heat press to the temperature shown in chart below.

Place the vinyl with the shiny carrier sheet side facing down on a machine mat and then use your cutting machine to **cut your desired pattern out of the vinyl. Weed as necessary** to remove any excess vinyl from the design.

Use a lint roller to remove any dust or debris from the felt.

Place your felt on top of the pressing pad.

Pre-press your felt for 10 seconds to remove any moisture and wrinkles.

Place the vinyl on the felt with the carrier sheet facing up.

Optionally, place the cover sheet over the top of the vinyl carrier sheet to avoid overheating the vinyl.

Press according to the chart below.

Allow to cool to the touch before slowly removing the carrier sheet.

Layer stack (top to bottom):
- heat source
- cover sheet
- HTV with carrier sheet side up
- felt
- pressing pad
- work surface

COOL PEEL

COOK TIMES
Here are typical times you can use as a starting point. Always check the manufacturer's instructions for time and temperature, when available.

your favorite settings

Traditional Heat Press	AutoPress	EasyPress	Mini Press	
280°F / 138°C	280°F / 138°C	280°F / 138°C	Medium	
10 seconds	10 seconds	15 seconds	15 seconds	
50 psi (Firm pressure)	Auto pressure	Firm pressure	Firm pressure	

TIPS & TRICKS
✓ Don't forget to mirror your design if your design has words or phrases.
✓ The carrier sheet should hold the vinyl in place; however, you can use heat-resistant tape to secure if needed.
✓ Flocked vinyl has a suede type texture and can be layered on top of a variety of heat transfer vinyl products.
✗ Do not wash your item for at least 24 hours after applying the HTV. If possible, turn item inside out before washing.

FLOCKED HTV

POLYESTER

Blanket, backpack, dress, hoodie, infant bodysuit, long-sleeved shirt, lounge pants, pajamas, pillowcase, plushie, polo shirt, shorts, tank top, t-shirt

Polyester is a blend of synthetic materials and is one of the most commonly used materials for textiles. Heat transfer vinyl is easily applied with low heat and medium to firm pressure.

INGREDIENTS
☐ Flocked heat transfer vinyl
☐ Base material, such as polyester blanket
☐ Cover sheet

EQUIPMENT
☐ Weeding tool
☐ Lint roller
☐ Flat heat source such as a heat press

PREPARATION

Start with a new polyester item, such as a blanket, for the best results. No need to pre-wash, but if you do, avoid fabric softener.

Pre-heat your flat heat press to the temperature listed below.

Place the vinyl with the shiny carrier sheet side facing down on a machine mat and then use your cutting machine to **cut your desired pattern out of the vinyl. Weed as necessary** to remove any excess vinyl from the design.

Place the polyester material on the pressing pad.

Using the lint roller, remove any debris or loose fibers from the blanket.

Cover the polyester material with a cover sheet and **pre-press for 5 seconds** to remove moisture and wrinkles. Then remove the cover sheet.

Place the vinyl on the polyester material with the carrier sheet facing up.

Replace the cover sheet over the carrier sheet to protect the vinyl and the polyester from overheating.

Press according to the chart below.

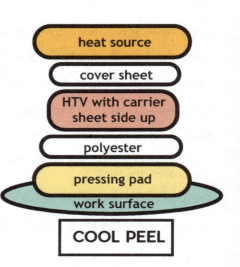

Allow to cool to the touch before **slowly removing the carrier sheet.**

COOK TIMES
Here are typical times you can use as a starting point. Always check the manufacturer's instructions for time and temperature, when available.

your favorite settings

Traditional Heat Press	AutoPress	EasyPress	Mini Press	
305°F / 152°C	305°F / 152°C	305°F / 152°C	Medium	
15 seconds	15 seconds	15 seconds	15 seconds	
50 psi (Firm pressure)	Auto pressure	Firm pressure	Firm pressure	

TIPS & TRICKS
✗ Do not wash your item for at least 24 hours after applying the HTV. If you wash a garment, turn it inside out first.
✓ You can apply vinyl designs to both sides of the blanket. Allow the first side to cool completely before applying vinyl to the second side.
✓ If the vinyl pulls from the blanket while removing the carrier sheet, carefully replace carrier sheet and apply a little more heat and pressure.

FLOCKED HTV

ATHLETIC MESH/JERSEY
Athletic skirt, athletic jersey, athletic shirt, athletic shorts

Athletic mesh fabric is durable and is commonly used for sports jerseys. The material comes in both micro-mesh and standard mesh sizes, providing a little bit of diversity in aesthetics.

INGREDIENTS
☐ Flocked heat transfer vinyl
☐ Base material, such as athletic skirt
☐ Cover sheet

EQUIPMENT
☐ Weeding tool
☐ Lint roller
☐ Flat heat source such as a heat press

PREPARATION

Start with new athletic mesh/jersey item, such as a skirt, for the best results. No need to pre-wash, but if you do, avoid fabric softener.

Pre-heat your flat heat press to the temperature listed below.

Place the vinyl with the shiny carrier sheet side facing down on a machine mat and then use your cutting machine to **cut your desired pattern out of the vinyl. Weed as necessary** to remove any excess vinyl from the design.

Place the athletic mesh onto the pressing pad.

Use a lint roller to remove any dust or fibers from the athletic mesh.

Cover the athletic mesh with a cover sheet and **pre-press for 5 seconds** to remove moisture and wrinkles. Remove the cover sheet.

Place the vinyl on the athletic mesh with the carrier sheet facing up.

Place a cover sheet over the carrier sheet to protect the vinyl and the athletic mesh from overheating.

Press according to the chart below.

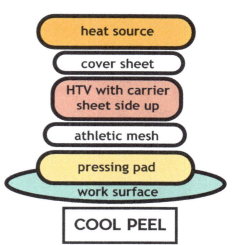

Once you have applied the appropriate amount of heat and pressure, **allow to cool before peeling the carrier sheet.**

COOK TIMES
Here are typical times you can use as a starting point. Always check the manufacturer's instructions for time and temperature, when available.

your favorite settings

Traditional Heat Press	AutoPress	EasyPress	Mini Press	
305°F / 152°C	305°F / 152°C	305°F / 152°C	Medium	
15 seconds	15 seconds	15 seconds	15 seconds	
50 psi (Firm pressure)	Auto pressure	Firm pressure	Firm pressure	

TIPS & TRICKS
✗ Do not wash your item for at least 24 hours after applying the HTV. If you wash a garment, turn it inside out first.
✓ Flocked vinyl has a suede type texture and can often be layered on other types of heat transfer vinyl for different effects.

EVERYTHING ELSE (HACKS FOR HTV)

CHAPTER 12
EVERYTHING ELSE (HACKS FOR HTV)

EVERYTHING ELSE (HACKS FOR HTV)

PRINTABLE HTV FOR LIGHT MATERIALS
ON COTTON, POLYESTER, CANVAS, NYLON

Printable HTV for light materials is designed for use on white and very light pastel materials. The recipe below uses a white long-sleeved shirt, but works for any light fabric blank.

INGREDIENTS
- ☐ Printable heat transfer sheet for light materials
- ☐ Base material, such as white long-sleeved shirt
- ☐ Cover sheet

EQUIPMENT
- ☐ Lint roller
- ☐ Weeding tool
- ☐ Flat heat source such as a heat press
- ☐ (Optional) T-shirt ruler for placement help
- ☐ (Optional) Heat-resistant tape

PREPARATION

Start with a new cotton, polyester, canvas, or nylon item, such as a cotton long-sleeved shirt, for the best results. No need to pre-wash, but if you do, avoid fabric softener.

Use a lint roller to remove any dust or debris from the base material.

Pre-heat your flat heat press to the temperature shown in chart below.

If using a shirt, fold the shirt in half lengthwise so both sides match up, then **pre-press for 10 seconds.** This both pre-heats the shirt to remove moisture and gives you a straight vertical crease for alignment. Unfold the shirt. Otherwise, just pre-press your base material for 10 seconds.

Use your inkjet printer to print your design onto a sheet of printable HTV for light colors. **Remember to mirror your design.**

If using the Print Then Cut feature in your design software, place your printable HTV face up on a machine mat and then using your cutting machine, **cut your design out. Weed as necessary.** If not using Print Then Cut, simply use scissors to cut out your design.

Place your design face down on your base material. Optionally, use heat-resistant tape to secure the printable HTV in place. **Cover the printable HTV** with a cover sheet.

Press according to the chart below.

Immediately remove the cover sheet and peel the backing away while still warm.

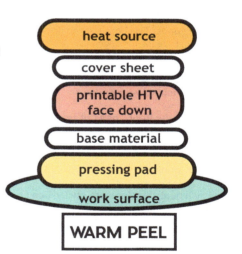

COOK TIMES
Here are typical times you can use as a starting point. Always check the manufacturer's instructions for time and temperature, when available.

your favorite settings

Traditional Heat Press	AutoPress	EasyPress	Mini Press	
375°F / 191°C	375°F / 191°C	375°F / 191°C	High	
30 seconds	30 seconds	30 seconds	30 seconds	
50 psi (Firm pressure)	Auto pressure	Firm pressure	Firm pressure	

TIPS & TRICKS
- ✓ Printable HTV will last for about 30 washes on gentle cycle. If you wash a garment, turn it inside out first.
- ✓ For a tutorial on printable HTV, check out jennifermaker.com/how-to-use-printable-vinyl-with-cricut

EVERYTHING ELSE (HACKS FOR HTV)

PRINTABLE HTV FOR DARK MATERIALS
ON COTTON, POLYESTER, CANVAS, NYLON

Printable HTV for dark materials is designed for use on materials of any color, light or dark. The recipe below is for a hoodie of any color, but works for any fabric blank.

INGREDIENTS
- ☐ Printable heat transfer sheet for dark materials
- ☐ Base material, such as a hoodie of any color
- ☐ Cover sheet
- ☐ Heat transfer mask

EQUIPMENT
- ☐ Lint roller
- ☐ Weeding tool
- ☐ Flat heat source such as a heat press
- ☐ (Optional) Ruler for placement help
- ☐ (Optional) Scraper

PREPARATION

Start with a new cotton, polyester, canvas, or nylon item, such as a cotton/polyester blend hoodie, for the best results. No need to pre-wash, but if you do, avoid fabric softener. **Use a lint roller** to remove any dust or debris from the hoodie.

Pre-heat your flat heat press to the temperature shown in chart below.

If using a shirt, fold it in in half lengthwise so both sides match up, then **pre-press for 10 seconds.** This both pre-heats the hoodie to remove moisture and gives you a straight vertical crease for alignment. **Unfold the hoodie.** Otherwise, just pre-press your base material for 10 seconds.

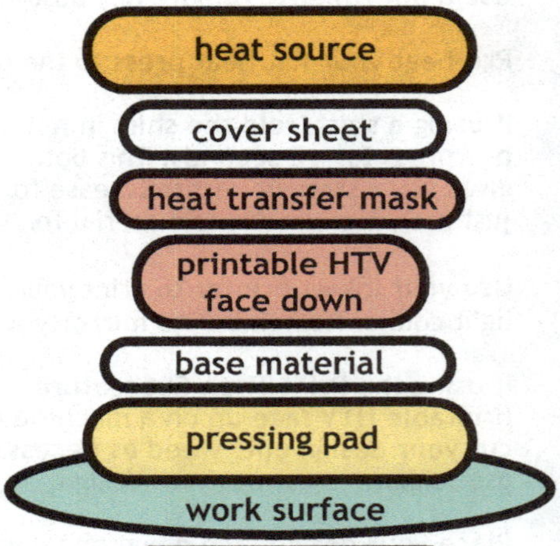

Use your inkjet printer to print your design onto a sheet of printable HTV for dark colors. **Do not mirror your design.**

If using the Print Then Cut feature in your design software, place your printable HTV face up on a machine mat and then using your cutting machine, **cut your design out.** Weed as necessary.

If not using Print Then Cut, simply use scissors to cut out your design.

Lay a heat transfer mask sticky-side up on your work surface. Carefully **lay your printable HTV face down on top,** starting from the center and working your way out to the edges. **Use a scraper** to make sure it adheres well. Then, carefully **peel the backing off the HTV.**

Place the printable HTV on the base material so your design is face up. The heat transfer mask should be face up as well. **Cover** the heat transfer mask and printable HTV with a cover sheet.

Press according to the chart below. Remove the cover sheet and let cool completely. Peel away the heat transfer mask.

Layer stack (top to bottom):
- heat source
- cover sheet
- heat transfer mask
- printable HTV face down
- base material
- pressing pad
- work surface

COOL PEEL

COOK TIMES
Here are typical times you can use as a starting point. Always check the manufacturer's instructions for time and temperature, when available.

Traditional Heat Press	AutoPress	EasyPress	Mini Press	your favorite settings
350°F / 177°C	350°F / 177°C	350°F / 177°C	Medium	
30 seconds	30 seconds	30 seconds	30 seconds	
40 psi (Medium pressure)	Auto pressure	Medium pressure	Medium pressure	

TIPS & TRICKS
- ✓ Wash inside out on gentle cycle. Dry on gentle cycle or air dry. If you wash a garment, turn it inside out first.
- ✓ For a tutorial on printable HTV, check out jennifermaker.com/how-to-use-printable-vinyl-with-cricut

EVERYTHING ELSE (HACKS FOR HTV)

COLORSPARK HTV
ON METAL, CERAMIC, PLASTIC, ACRYLIC, GLASS

ColorSpark HTV allows you to make decals and stickers with heat transfer vinyl. The recipe below is for a metal tumbler, but ColorSpark HTV can be used to put decals on tumblers, cups, and more. For the recipe example below, be sure to use a Mini Press, as a traditional heat press or AutoPress will NOT work.

INGREDIENTS
- ☐ ColorSpark heat transfer vinyl
- ☐ Any heat transfer vinyl, such as glitter or holographic
- ☐ Base material, such as metal tumbler
- ☐ Cover sheets
- ☐ Heat transfer mask

EQUIPMENT
- ☐ Microfiber cloth
- ☐ Rubbing alcohol
- ☐ Weeding tool
- ☐ Heat source such as a heat press
- ☐ (Optional) Ruler for placement help

PREPARATION

Start with a new metal, ceramic, plastic, acrylic, or glass item, such as a metal tumbler.

Use a microfiber cloth and rubbing alcohol to clean the outside of your metal tumbler. Let dry completely.

Pre-heat your heat press to the temperature shown in the chart below.

Cut the Colorspark HTV. Make sure this is NOT mirrored. Place the vinyl **shiny side up** and then use your cutting machine to **cut your desired pattern** out of the vinyl. **Weed as necessary** to remove excess vinyl.

Cut the other HTV of your choice. Make sure this is mirrored. Place the vinyl **carrier sheet side down on a machine mat** and then use your cutting machine to cut your desired pattern out of the vinyl. **Weed as necessary** to remove any excess vinyl from the design.

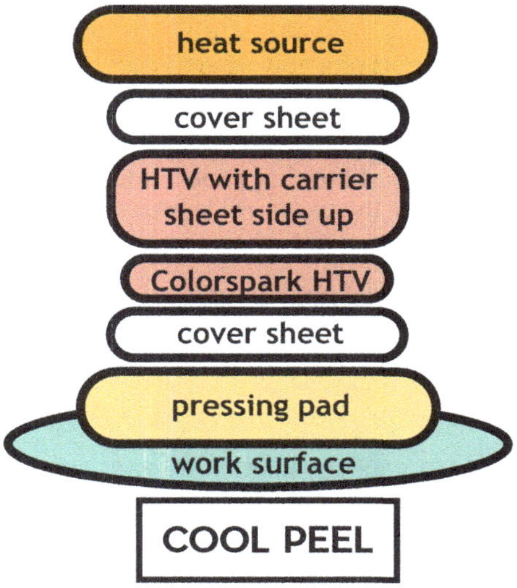

Place a cover sheet down on pressing pad, then **place the ColorSpark HTV face up** the on cover sheet.

Lay your other HTV face down on top of the ColorSpark HTV. Make sure it is aligned properly. **Place another cover sheet** on top of everything.

Press according to the chart below. **For the tumbler do not use the traditional press, autopress, or easy press, these presses are for flat materials only.**

Allow to cool completely, then remove cover sheet.

Place transfer mask sticky side up on your work surface. **Place your decal face down on top,** starting in the center and working your way to the edges. Use a scraper to adhere it well. **Remove the backing on the decal.**

Apply the decal to the metal tumbler, starting in the center and working your way to the edges. Use a scraper to adhere it well. **Peel off the transfer mask.**

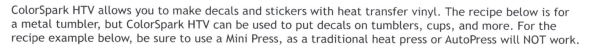

COOL PEEL

COOK TIMES
Here are typical times you can use as a starting point. Always check the manufacturer's instructions for time and temperature, when available.

your favorite settings

Traditional Heat Press	AutoPress	EasyPress	Mini Press	
305°F / 152°C	305°F / 152°C	305°F / 152°C	Medium	
8 seconds	8 seconds	8 seconds	8 seconds	
40 psi (Medium pressure)	Auto pressure	Medium pressure	Medium pressure	

TIPS & TRICKS
✓ If using as a sticker rather than a decal, transfer mask is not needed. Simply peel it up off the backing.

EVERYTHING ELSE (HACKS FOR HTV)

CLEAR HTV FOR SUBLIMATION
ON FABRIC, WOOD, GLASS, CANVAS

Certain types of HTV are coated in a polymer that allows them to accept sublimation ink. Sublimating on HTV allows you to apply a sublimation print to materials that do not normally allow for sublimation. This recipe is for clear HTV in a matte or glossy finish on a 100% cotton shirt, but it can be used on other fabric, wood, glass, and canvas.

INGREDIENTS
- ☐ Clear heat transfer vinyl
- ☐ Base material, such as 100% cotton shirt
- ☐ Blowout paper (uncoated butcher paper)
- ☐ Mirrored sublimation transfer (print/sheet)

EQUIPMENT
- ☐ Lint roller
- ☐ Weeding tool
- ☐ Heat-resistant tape
- ☐ Flat heat source such as a heat press
- ☐ (Optional) T-shirt ruler for placement help
- ☐ (Optional) Pillow or foam insert

PREPARATION

Start with a new fabric, wood, glass, or canvas item, such as a cotton fabric shirt, for the best results. No need to pre-wash. Lint roll your shirt to remove any dust and debris.

Pre-heat your flat heat press to 320°F / 160°C.

Cut away any excess vinyl material and weed your design. You may choose to use scissors or a cutting machine. If using a cutting machine, **place your vinyl on a machine mat** and **cut your desired pattern** out of your vinyl.

If using a shirt, **pre-press the shirt for 10 seconds** to remove moisture. Then, **slide a piece of blowout paper inside your shirt.** Optionally, you can also place a pressing pillow under the paper inside your shirt. Otherwise, just pre-press your base material for 10 seconds.

Align and place your vinyl onto the base material. Keep the shiny carrier sheet side facing up. **Press to tack down the vinyl** for 15 seconds. **Allow to cool** before removing carrier sheet.

Increase the heat of your press to the temperature listed in the chart below.

Cut your sublimation transfer print to align with the size and shape of the HTV. You can choose to trim closely with scissors or a cutting machine.

Align your **sublimation transfer sheet face down** on top of the vinyl and **secure it with heat-resistant tape.** Place a sheet of blowout paper on top of the transfer sheet.

Press according to the chart below.

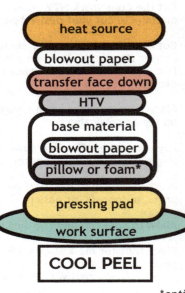

*optional

COOK TIMES
Here are typical times you can use as a starting point. Always check the manufacturer's instructions for time and temperature, when available.

your favorite settings

Traditional Heat Press	AutoPress	EasyPress	Mini Press	
385°F / 196°C	400°F / 204°C	385°F / 196°C	Medium	
45-60 seconds	45 seconds	40 seconds	50 seconds	
30 psi (Light pressure)	Auto pressure	Light pressure	Light pressure	

TIPS & TRICKS
✓ For projects and a tutorial, check out jennifermaker.com/how-to-sublimate-clear-htv

EVERYTHING ELSE (HACKS FOR HTV)

GLITTER HTV FOR SUBLIMATION
ON COTTON, POLY-BLENDS, CANVAS, WOOD, GLASS

Certain types of HTV are coated in a polymer that allows them to accept sublimation ink. Sublimating on HTV allows you to apply a sublimation print to materials that do not normally allow for sublimation. Glitter HTV will adhere to cotton, canvas, wood, glass, and more.

INGREDIENTS
- ☐ Glitter heat transfer vinyl
- ☐ Base material, such as polyester blend makeup bag
- ☐ Blowout paper (uncoated butcher paper)
- ☐ Mirrored sublimation transfer (print/sheet)

EQUIPMENT
- ☐ Lint roller
- ☐ Weeding tool
- ☐ Heat-resistant tape
- ☐ Flat heat source such as a heat press
- ☐ (Optional) Ruler for placement help
- ☐ (Optional) Pillow or foam insert

PREPARATION

Start with a new cotton, polyester blend, canvas, wood, or glass item, such as a polyester blend makeup bag, for the best results. No need to pre-wash. **Lint roll** your shirt to remove any dust and debris.

Pre-heat your flat heat press to 320°F / 160°C.

Cut away any excess vinyl material and weed your design. You may choose to use scissors or a cutting machine. If using a cutting machine, **place your vinyl on a machine mat** and **cut your desired pattern** out of your vinyl.

Pre-press the base material for **10 seconds** to remove moisture.

Optionally, slide a piece of blowout paper (I recommend cardstock) **inside your base material.** Optionally, you can also place a pressing pillow under the paper inside your base material.

Align and place your vinyl onto the base material. Keep the shiny carrier sheet side facing up. **Press to tack down the vinyl for 15 seconds. Allow to cool** before removing the carrier sheet.

Increase the heat of your press to the temperature listed in the chart below.

Cut your sublimation transfer print to align with the size and shape of the HTV. You can choose to trim closely with scissors or a cutting machine.

Align your **sublimation transfer sheet face down** on top of the vinyl and **secure it with heat-resistant tape**. **Place a sheet of blowout paper** on top of the transfer sheet.

Press according to the chart below.

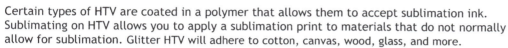

Stack (top to bottom): heat source / blowout paper / transfer face down / glitter HTV / base material / blowout paper / pressing pad / work surface — **COOL PEEL**

COOK TIMES
Here are typical times you can use as a starting point. Always check the manufacturer's instructions for time and temperature, when available.

your favorite settings

Traditional Heat Press	AutoPress	EasyPress	Mini Press	
400°F / 204°C	400°F / 204°C	385°F / 196°C	Medium	
35-40 seconds	35-40 seconds	40 seconds	50 seconds	
30 psi (Light pressure)	Auto pressure	Light pressure	Light pressure	

TIPS & TRICKS
- ✗ Do not wash your item for at least 24 hours after applying the HTV. If you wash a garment, turn it inside out first.
- ✓ For projects and a tutorial, check out jennifermaker.com/how-to-sublimate-on-cotton

EVERYTHING ELSE (HACKS FOR HTV)

HOLOGRAPHIC HTV FOR SUBLIMATION
ON COTTON, POLYESTER, POLY-BLENDS, SPANDEX

Certain types of HTV are coated in a polymer that allows them to accept sublimation ink. Sublimating on HTV allows you to apply a sublimation print to materials that do not normally allow for sublimation. This recipe is for a dark colored polyester car flag, but holographic HTV will also adhere to cotton, poly-cotton blends, and some spandex materials.

INGREDIENTS
☐ Holographic heat transfer vinyl
☐ Base material, such as dark colored polyester car flag
☐ Blowout paper (uncoated butcher paper)
☐ Sublimation transfer (print/sheet)

EQUIPMENT
☐ Lint roller
☐ Weeding tool
☐ Heat-resistant tape
☐ Flat heat source such as a heat press
☐ (Optional) Ruler for placement help

PREPARATION

Start with a new cotton, polyester, or spandex item, such as a polyester car flag, for the best results. No need to pre-wash. **Lint roll** your shirt to remove any dust and debris.

Pre-heat your flat heat press to 320°F / 160°C.

Cut away any excess vinyl material and weed your design. You may choose to use scissors or a cutting machine. If using a cutting machine, **place your vinyl on a machine mat** and **cut your desired pattern** out of your vinyl.

Place a sheet of blowout paper on top of the base material and pre-press for 10 seconds to remove moisture, then remove the blowout paper.

Slide a piece of blowout paper underneath the base material

Align and place your vinyl onto the base material. Keep the shiny carrier sheet side facing up. **Place a sheet of blowout paper** on top. **Press to tack down the vinyl** for 10 seconds. **Allow to cool** before removing the carrier sheet.

Increase the heat of your press to the temperature listed in the chart below.

Cut your sublimation transfer print to align with the size and shape of the HTV. You can choose to trim closely with scissors or a cutting machine.

Align your **sublimation transfer sheet face down** on top of the vinyl and **secure it with heat-resistant tape. Place a sheet of blowout paper** on top of the transfer sheet.

Press according to the chart below.

Stack diagram:
- heat source
- blowout paper
- transfer face down
- holographic HTV
- base material
- blowout paper
- pressing pad
- work surface

COOL PEEL

COOK TIMES
Here are typical times you can use as a starting point. Always check the manufacturer's instructions for time and temperature, when available.

Traditional Heat Press	AutoPress	EasyPress	Mini Press	your favorite settings
380°F / 193°C	380°F / 193°C	380°F / 193°C	High	
40 seconds	40 seconds	40 seconds	50 seconds	
30 psi (Light pressure)	Auto pressure	Light pressure	Light pressure	

TIPS & TRICKS
✓ For projects and a tutorial, check out jennifermaker.com/how-to-sublimate-on-cotton

GLOW-IN-THE-DARK HTV FOR SUBLIMATION

COTTON, POLYESTER, POLY-BLENDS, FAUX LEATHER

Certain types of HTV are coated in a polymer that allows them to accept sublimation ink. Sublimating on HTV allows you to apply a sublimation print to materials that do not normally allow for sublimation. This recipe is for a 100% cotton sweatshirt, but glow-in-the-dark HTV can also adhere to polyester, poly-blends, and faux leather.

INGREDIENTS

- ☐ Glow in the dark heat transfer vinyl
- ☐ Base material, such as 100% cotton sweatshirt
- ☐ Blowout paper (uncoated butcher paper)
- ☐ Sublimation transfer (print/sheet)

EQUIPMENT

- ☐ Lint roller
- ☐ Weeding tool
- ☐ Heat-resistant tape
- ☐ Flat heat source such as a heat press
- ☐ (Optional) T-shirt ruler for placement help
- ☐ (Optional) Pillow or foam insert

PREPARATION

Start with a new cotton, polyester, or faux leather item, such as a cotton sweatshirt, for the best results. No need to pre-wash. **Lint roll** your sweatshirt to remove any debris.

Pre-heat your flat heat press to 305°F / 151°C.

Cut away any excess vinyl material and weed your design. You may choose to use scissors or a cutting machine. If using a cutting machine, **place your vinyl on a machine mat** and **cut your desired pattern** out of your vinyl.

Pre-press the base material for 10 seconds to remove moisture. Then, optionally, **slide a piece of blowout paper inside your** base material. Optionally, you can also place a pressing pillow under the paper inside your base material.

Align and place your vinyl onto the base material. Keep the shiny carrier sheet side facing up. **Press to tack down the vinyl** for 5 seconds. **Allow to cool** before removing carrier sheet.

Increase the heat of your press to the temperature listed in the chart below.

Cut your sublimation transfer print to align with the size and shape of the HTV. You can choose to trim closely with scissors or a cutting machine.

Align your **sublimation transfer sheet face down** on top of the vinyl and **secure it with heat-resistant tape. Place a sheet of blowout paper** on top of the transfer sheet.

Press according to the chart below.

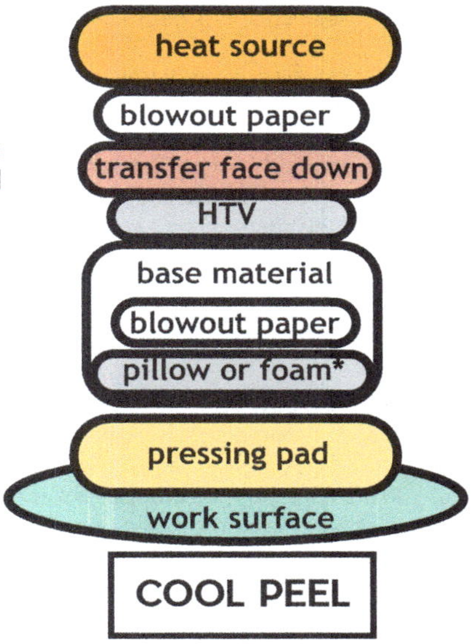
heat source
blowout paper
transfer face down
HTV
base material
blowout paper
pillow or foam*
pressing pad
work surface
COOL PEEL

*optional

COOK TIMES

Here are typical times you can use as a starting point. Always check the manufacturer's instructions for time and temperature, when available.

your favorite settings

Traditional Heat Press	AutoPress	EasyPress	Mini Press	
355°F / 179°C	355°F / 179°C	325°F / 163°C	Medium	
70 seconds	70 seconds	70 seconds	80 seconds	
30 psi (Light pressure)	Auto pressure	Light pressure	Light pressure	

TIPS & TRICKS

✓ For projects and a tutorial, check out jennifermaker.com/how-to-sublimate-on-cotton

EVERYTHING ELSE (HACKS FOR HTV)

EASYSUBLI
COTTON, POLYESTER, POLY-BLENDS, CERAMIC, METAL, PLASTIC, ACRYLIC, WOOD

Siser EasySubli is designed to be used with sublimation and comes with heat-resistant mask transfer tape. This recipe is for a cotton t-shirt, but EasySubli can be used on almost any blank that accepts vinyl and HTV.

INGREDIENTS
- ☐ Base material, such as a blank cotton t-shirt
- ☐ Siser EasySubli (one sheet)
- ☐ Blowout paper (uncoated butcher paper) (two sheets)
- ☐ Sublimation transfer (print/sheet)
- ☐ (Optional) EasySubli mask transfer tape

EQUIPMENT
- ☐ Lint roller
- ☐ Weeding tool
- ☐ Flat heat source such as a heat press
- ☐ Heat-resistant tape
- ☐ (Optional) T-shirt ruler for placement help
- ☐ (Optional) Pillow or foam insert

PREPARATION

Start with a new cotton, polyester, ceramic, metal, plastic, acrylic, or wood item, such as a cotton T-shirt, for the best results. No need to pre-wash, but if you do, avoid fabric softener. Use a lint roller to clean the surface of your shirt.

Pre-heat your flat heat press to the temperature shown in the chart below.

Lay your base material on the pressing pad. **Pre-press for 10 seconds** to eliminate any moisture.

Cut your print-then-cut sublimation transfer and EasySubli shape. Make sure the transfer is mirrored, but the EasySubli shape is not. Weed the transfer. Weed and closely trim the EasySubli shape.

Lay the EasySubli shape with the carrier sheet facing down on your work surface. Peel the mask transfer tape from the backing and apply it to the EasySubli shape. Use a scraper to smooth out any bubbles and creases.

Peel the EasySubli shape away from the carrier sheet. The mask is not necessary if your shape is solid and not complicated.

Place a sheet of blowout paper (I recommend cardstock) inside the base material, if possible. **Place the EasySubli shape on the base material face down.** Cover with blowout paper. Press for 5 seconds to tack the EasySubli to the base material. Remove the blowout paper. If using a mask, peel the it off while still warm.

Place the sublimation transfer face down on the EasySubli, making sure it is aligned properly. Secure in place with heat-resistant tape. Cover with another sheet of blowout paper.

Press according to the chart below. Pull the transfer sheet while still warm.

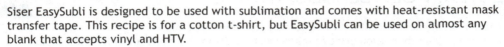

Stack (top to bottom): heat source / blowout paper / transfer face down / EasySubli / base material / blowout paper / pillow or foam* / pressing pad / work surface

WARM PEEL

* optional

COOK TIMES
Here are typical times you can use as a starting point. Always check the manufacturer's instructions for time and temperature, when available.

your favorite settings

Traditional Heat Press	AutoPress	EasyPress	Mini Press	
385°F / 196°C	385°F / 196°C	385°F / 196°C	High	
40 seconds	40 seconds	40 seconds	50 seconds	
30 psi (Light pressure)	Auto pressure	Light pressure	Light pressure	

TIPS & TRICKS
✓ For a tutorial check out jennifermaker.com/how-to-sublimate-on-cotton

HTV COOKBOOK

BEYOND THE RECIPES

WORKSHEETS & NOTES

These worksheets help you track important things for your projects.

Feel free to make as many copies of them as you need!

MY PROJECT NOTES

HTV COOKBOOK

MY PROJECT NOTES

MY PROJECT NOTES

MY PROJECT NOTES

HTV COOKBOOK

MY FAVORITES

Vinyl Cutting Machine
- _____

Heat Transfer Vinyl Brands
- _____
- _____
- _____

Heat Transfer Vinyl Types
- _____
- _____
- _____
- _____

Base Materials
- _____
- _____
- _____
- _____
- _____

Cover Sheet and Brands
- _____
- _____
- _____
- _____

Websites for HTV Supplies
- _____
- _____
- _____
- _____
- _____
- _____

HTV COOKBOOK

INDEX

A
Activewear 18, 35, 42, 104
Adhesive 4, 9, 10, 26, 38
Art canvas 24, 43, 53, 64, 73, 82, 98, 108
Athletic jersey 32, 117
Athletic mesh 3, 32, 117
Athletic shirt 32, 117
Athletic shorts 32, 39, 117
Athletic skirt 32, 39, 117
Autopress 5, 65

B
Backdrop 24, 43, 53, 64, 73, 82, 98, 108
Backpack 16, 18, 33, 35, 37, 42, 46, 50, 63, 70, 79, 88, 91, 97, 104, 110, 116
Bag 13, 18, 22, 23, 24, 25, 28, 30, 35, 37, 38, 41, 42, 43, 48, 53, 54, 55, 59, 64, 67, 73, 76, 82, 83, 84, 91, 93, 98, 100, 101, 103, 104, 108, 109, 115, 123
Baggage tag 25, 54, 83, 103
Baking tray 20, 66
Banner 23, 41, 55, 101
Basket 22, 109, 115
Bike shorts 34, 114
Bin 20, 66
Blade 12
Blanket 15, 16, 17, 33, 36, 44, 45, 46, 50, 51, 52, 62, 63, 70, 71, 72, 78, 79, 81, 86, 88, 89, 90, 95, 96, 97, 106, 107, 110, 112, 113, 116
Blowout paper 5, 122, 124, 125, 126
Bookmark 25, 54, 83, 103
Brayer 12
Bucket 20, 66
Bunting 22, 23, 41, 55, 101, 109, 115
Burlap 3, 23, 41, 55, 101
Burp cloth 15, 17, 36, 44, 45, 51, 52, 62, 71, 72, 78, 81, 86, 89, 90, 95, 96, 106, 107, 112, 113
Butcher paper 5, 6, 122, 124, 125, 126

C
Candle holder 19
Canvas 3, 24, 43, 53, 64, 73, 82, 98, 108
Car coaster 38
Cardboard 21, 56
Cardstock 3, 4, 7, 21, 56, 126
Cardstock card 21, 56
Ceramic 3, 29, 30, 60, 68
Chameleon 3, 86
Chapstick holder 28, 38, 48, 59, 67, 76, 84, 93, 100
Charcuterie board 26, 47, 57, 74, 80, 92, 99
Clear heat transfer vinyl 122
Coaster 27, 28, 29, 38, 48, 58, 59, 67, 75, 76, 84, 85, 93, 100, 102
ColorSpark heat transfer vinyl 121
Cooler 24, 43, 53, 64, 73, 82, 98, 108
Cool peel 15, 16, 17, 18, 19, 20, 24, 26, 28, 32, 33, 34, 35, 36, 37, 38, 39, 43, 44, 45, 46, 47, 48, 50, 51, 52, 53, 54, 55, 56, 57, 58, 59, 60, 62, 63, 64, 67, 68, 70, 71, 72, 73, 74, 75, 76, 78, 79, 80, 81, 82, 83, 84, 85, 86, 88, 89, 90, 91, 92, 93, 95, 96, 97, 98, 99, 100, 101, 102, 103, 104, 112, 113, 114, 115, 116, 117, 120, 121, 122, 123, 124, 125
Corkboard 3, 27, 58, 102, 133
Cosmetic bag 25, 54, 64, 83, 103
Cotton 3, 17, 24, 36, 43, 45, 52, 62, 72, 78, 81, 89, 90, 95, 96, 106, 107, 112, 113
Cotton/Poly Blend 3
Cover Sheet 6
Cricut 2, 5, 7, 12, 135, 136, 141
Curved surface 19, 20, 65, 66
Cut setting 11
Cutting board 6, 21, 26, 47, 56, 57, 74, 80, 92, 99, 106, 107, 109, 110
Cutting Machine 5, 132
Cutting Tips & Tricks 11

D
Denim jacket 106
Doorknob hanger 26, 47, 57, 74, 80, 92, 99
Doormat 91
Door sign 26, 47, 57, 74, 80, 92, 99
Drawstring bag 18, 35, 42, 104
Dress 15, 16, 17, 33, 34, 36, 37, 44, 45, 46, 50, 51, 52, 62, 63, 70, 71, 72, 78, 79, 81, 86, 88, 89, 90, 91, 95, 96, 97, 106, 107, 110, 112, 113, 114, 116
Drinking glass 19, 65
Drink sleeve 28, 38, 48, 59, 67, 76, 84, 93, 100

E
Earrings 25, 54, 83, 103
EasyPress 5
EasySubli 126

F
Faux Leather 3
Felt 3, 22, 109, 115
Flag 23, 24, 41, 43, 53, 55, 64, 73, 82, 98, 101, 108, 124
Flex/Stretch heat transfer vinyl 7, 32, 33, 34, 35, 36, 37, 38
Flip flops 28, 38, 48, 59, 67, 76, 84, 93, 100
Flocked heat transfer vinyl 8, 112, 113, 114, 115, 116, 117
Flowers 22, 109, 115
Foam, pressing 6
Foil heat transfer vinyl 8, 70
Furniture upholstery 30

G
Garden flag 23, 41, 55, 101
Glass 3, 19, 65
Glass block 19, 65
Glitter heat transfer vinyl 7, 62, 63, 64, 65, 66, 67, 68, 123
Gloves 6
Glow-in-the-dark heat transfer vinyl 8, 88, 89, 90, 91, 92, 93

HTV COOKBOOK

H
Headband 34, 114
Heat gun 5, 10
Heat-resistant gloves 5, 6, 20, 60, 65, 66, 68
Heat-resistant tape 6
Heat sources 5
Heat transfer mask 120, 121
Holographic heat transfer vinyl 7, 50, 51, 52, 53, 54, 55, 56, 57, 58, 59, 60, 124
Home decor 4, 22, 27, 58, 75, 85, 102, 109, 115
Hoodie 15, 16, 17, 33, 36, 44, 45, 46, 50, 51, 52, 62, 63, 70, 71, 72, 78, 79, 81, 86, 88, 89, 90, 95, 96, 97, 106, 107, 110, 112, 113, 116, 120
How to Layer HTV 13

I
Infant bodysuit 15, 16, 17, 33, 36, 37, 44, 45, 46, 50, 51, 52, 62, 63, 71, 72, 79, 81, 86, 89, 91, 95, 96, 97, 107, 110, 112, 113, 116
Iron 5, 10

J
Jacket, denim. See Denim jacket
Jerseys 32, 39, 117
Jogging shorts 42
Journal cover 25, 54, 83, 103

K
Keychain 20, 66
Kneeling pad 28, 38, 48, 59, 67, 76, 84, 93, 100

L
Lamp shade 22, 109, 115
Laptop sleeve 28, 38, 48, 59, 67, 76, 84, 93, 100
Leggings 34, 39, 114
Leotard 34, 39, 114
License plate 20, 66
License plate cover 20, 66
Lint roller 5, 6, 15, 16, 17, 18, 21, 22, 23, 24, 28, 30, 32, 33, 34, 35, 36, 37, 38, 39, 41, 42, 43, 44, 45, 46, 48, 50, 51, 52, 53, 55, 56, 58, 59, 62, 63, 64, 67, 70, 71, 72, 73, 75, 76, 78, 79, 81, 82, 84, 85, 86, 88, 89, 90, 91, 93, 95, 96, 97, 98, 100, 101, 102, 104, 106, 107, 109, 110, 112, 113, 114, 115, 116, 117, 119, 120, 122, 124, 125, 126
Long-sleeved shirt 15, 16, 17, 33, 36, 37, 44, 45, 46, 50, 51, 52, 62, 63, 70, 71, 72, 78, 79, 81, 86, 88, 89, 90, 91, 95, 96, 97, 106, 107, 110, 112, 116, 119
Lounge pants 15, 16, 17, 33, 36, 44, 45, 46, 50, 51, 52, 62, 63, 70, 71, 72, 78, 79, 81, 86, 88, 89, 90, 95, 96, 97, 106, 107, 110, 112, 113, 116
Lunch bag 28, 38, 48, 59, 67, 76, 84, 93, 100
Lunchbox 20, 66

M
Mesh heat transfer vinyl 7, 41, 42, 43, 44, 45, 46, 47, 48
Metal 3, 20, 66, 121
Metal, sheet 20, 66
Metal sign 20
Microfiber cloth 5, 6, 19, 20, 25, 26, 27, 29, 47, 54, 57, 60, 65, 66, 68, 74, 80, 83, 92, 99, 103, 108, 121
MiniPress 5
Mobile 22, 109, 115, 140
Mousepad 28, 38, 48, 59, 67, 76, 84, 93, 100
Mug 60, 68
Mug without handles 60, 68

N
Neoprene 3, 28, 38, 48, 59, 67, 76, 84, 93, 100
Non-woven 30
Notebook 2, 21, 25, 54, 56, 83, 103
Notebook cover 21, 56
Notecard 21, 56

Nylon
Nylon 3, 18, 35, 42, 104

O
Offset 11
Ornament 22, 109, 115
Oven 60, 68
Oven-safe tray 60, 68

P
Pad, pressing 5, 6
Paint 47, 74, 99
Pajamas 15, 16, 17, 33, 36, 44, 45, 46, 50, 51, 52, 62, 63, 70, 71, 72, 78, 79, 81, 86, 88, 89, 90, 95, 96, 97, 106, 107, 110, 112, 113, 116
Pane, glass 19, 65
Panel, glass 19, 65
Pants 15, 16, 17, 33, 36, 37, 44, 45, 46, 50, 51, 52, 62, 63, 70, 71, 72, 78, 79, 81, 86, 88, 89, 90, 91, 95, 96, 97, 106, 107, 110, 112, 113, 116
Paper, blowout. See Blowout paper
Parchment paper 5, 6
Patterned heat transfer vinyl 8, 78, 79, 80, 81, 82, 83, 84, 85
Pencil cup 60, 68
Performance wear 39
Pillowcase 15, 16, 17, 23, 33, 36, 41, 44, 45, 46, 50, 51, 52, 55, 62, 63, 70, 71, 72, 78, 79, 81, 86, 88, 89, 90, 95, 96, 97, 101, 106, 107, 110, 112, 113, 116
Pillow, pressing 5, 6, 15, 16, 17, 18, 22, 24, 25, 30, 32, 33, 34, 35, 36, 37, 43, 45, 46, 50, 51, 52, 53, 59, 62, 64, 71, 72, 78, 79, 81, 84, 88, 89, 90, 95, 96, 97, 98, 104, 109, 115, 122, 125, 126
Placemat 22, 24, 43, 53, 64, 73, 82, 98, 108, 109, 115
Plant fibers 23, 41, 55, 101
Plaque 19, 65
Plushie 15, 16, 17, 33, 36, 44, 45, 46, 50, 51, 52, 62, 63, 70, 71, 72, 78, 79, 81, 86, 88, 89, 90, 95, 96, 97, 106, 107, 110, 112, 113, 116

Polo shirt 15, 16, 17, 33, 36, 37, 44, 45, 46, 50, 51, 52, 62, 63, 70, 71, 72, 78, 79, 81, 86, 88, 89, 90, 91, 95, 96, 97, 106, 107, 110, 112, 113, 116
Polyester 3, 14, 31, 49, 61, 69, 77, 87, 94, 105, 111, 118
Poly/Nylon Blend 3
Polypropylene 30
Poncho 18, 35, 42, 104
Press, Auto. See AutoPress
Press, Easy. See EasyPress
Pressing pillow. See Pillow, pressing
Press, Mini. See MiniPress
Press, traditional heat. See Traditional heat press
Pressure 9
Pressure setting 9, 11
Printable heat transfer sheet 8, 119, 120
Print Then Cut 119, 120
Psi 9
Puff heat transfer vinyl 8, 106, 107, 108, 109, 110

R
Reverse art canvas 24, 43, 53, 64, 98, 108
Rubbing Alcohol 6
Ruler 5, 6, 18, 19, 20, 21, 22, 23, 24, 27, 28, 38, 39, 41, 53, 54, 55, 56, 57, 58, 59, 63, 64, 66, 74, 75, 80, 82, 83, 84, 85, 86, 91, 92, 95, 96, 97, 98, 99, 100, 101, 102, 103, 104, 109, 115, 120, 121, 124

S
Sail 24, 43, 53, 64, 73, 82, 98, 108
Sand paper 6
Sanitizer bottle holder 28, 38, 48, 67, 76, 84, 93, 100
Scraper 6
Serving tray 27, 58, 75, 85, 102
Setting, cut. See Cut setting
Setting, pressure. See Pressure setting
Sheet metal. See Metal, sheet

Shoes 24, 43, 53, 64, 73, 82, 98, 108
Shorts 15, 16, 17, 32, 33, 34, 36, 37, 39, 42, 44, 45, 46, 50, 51, 52, 62, 63, 70, 71, 72, 78, 79, 81, 86, 88, 89, 90, 91, 95, 96, 97, 106, 107, 110, 112, 113, 114, 116, 117
Sign 20, 26, 47, 57, 66, 74, 80, 92, 99
Siser EasySubli 126
Siser EasyWeed Stretch 3, 39
Siser EasyWeed Stretch heat transfer vinyl 39
Sleep mask 22, 109, 115
Spandex 3, 34, 114
Sportswear 30
Stain 74, 99
Standard heat transfer vinyl 7, 15, 16, 17, 18, 19, 20, 21, 22, 23, 24, 25, 26, 27, 28, 29, 30
Stretch Polyester 3
Sublimation transfer 124, 125, 126
Sublimation transfer, mirrored 122, 124, 125, 126
Sweatshirt 15, 17, 36, 44, 45, 51, 52, 62, 71, 72, 78, 81, 86, 89, 90, 95, 96, 106, 107, 112, 113, 125
Swimwear 18, 35, 42, 104
Synthetic 16, 18, 25, 28, 30, 33, 34, 35, 37, 38, 42, 46, 48, 50, 54, 59, 63, 67, 70, 76, 79, 83, 84, 88, 91, 93, 97, 100, 103, 104, 110, 114, 116

T
Table runner 23, 41, 55, 101
Tank top 15, 16, 17, 33, 34, 36, 37, 44, 45, 46, 50, 51, 52, 62, 63, 70, 71, 72, 78, 79, 81, 86, 88, 89, 90, 91, 95, 96, 97, 106, 107, 110, 112, 113, 114, 116
Tape. See heat-resistant tape
Tech accessory bag 18, 35, 42, 104
Teflon sheet 6
Temperature 10
Tent 24, 43, 53, 64, 73, 82, 98, 108
Tile 29, 63
Tote bag 24, 25, 37, 43, 53, 54, 64, 73, 82, 83, 91, 98, 103, 108

Traditional heat press 5, 38, 65, 66, 100, 121
Travel organizer 22, 109, 115
Trivet 27, 29, 58, 75, 85, 102
T-shirt 6, 15, 16, 17 33, 34, 36, 37, 44, 45, 46, 51, 52, 62, 63, 70, 71, 72, 78, 81, 86, 88, 89, 90, 91, 95, 96, 97, 106, 110, 112, 113, 114, 116, 126
Tumbler 20, 66, 121

U
Umbrella 18, 35, 42, 104
UV color change heat transfer vinyl 95, 96, 97, 98, 99, 100, 101, 102, 103, 104

V
Vase 19, 65

W
Wallet 25, 54, 83, 103
Warm peel 22, 23, 25, 27, 29, 30, 41, 42, 65, 66, 106, 107, 108, 109, 110, 119, 126
Waterproof 4
Weeding box 11
Weeding tool 6
Windbreaker 18, 35, 42, 104
Wine bag 23, 41, 55, 101
Wood 3, 26, 47, 57, 74, 80, 92, 99, 106, 109, 110
Wreath 23, 41, 55, 101

Y
Yard sign 26, 47, 57, 74, 80, 92, 99
Yoga block 27, 58, 75, 85, 102

Z
Zipper pouch 64

SAVE ON HTV SUPPLIES

I can get you a 10% discount on Cricut supplies and materials when you order over $100 of these items from the Cricut Shop... plus free shipping in the U.S. The discount changes frequently, so to get the latest code please go to this link:

https://jennifermaker.com/cricutdiscount

Don't know where to start? Check out my favorite accessories at
jennifermaker.com/what-cricut-accessories-need

Recommendations for Cricut blades, weeding tools, heat presses, machine mats, and more!

HTV COOKBOOK

NEED SOME CHEATSHEETS?
GET THE CRICUT COACH PLAYBOOK

Become a Cricut Expert with my step-by-step playbook for all the popular tasks in Cricut Design Space!

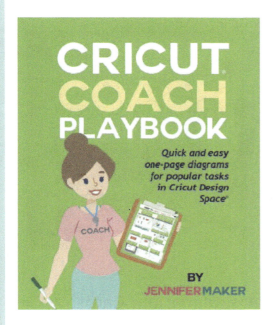

Can't remember how to do print then cut? Not sure how to remove a background from an uploaded image? Clueless about Snapmat and how it can help? The Cricut Coach Playbook can help, with over 100 step-by-step diagrams. Each of these "cheat sheets" show you exactly what to click and what to do for easy, fast results.

By learning in small steps, you avoid the overwhelm that usually comes with trying to get control over something that is confusing and hard-to-remember.

The Cricut Coach Playbook is a collection of step-by-step diagrams with easy-to-follow directions for all the most popular tasks in Cricut Design Space! It tells you exactly what to do for each task. If you just want someone to tell you what to do, this is it.

Used by more than 400,000 Cricut owners!

Learn more and get your copy today at jennifermaker.com/cricutcoach

HTV COOKBOOK

GET STARTED WITH SUBLIMATION COOKBOOK!

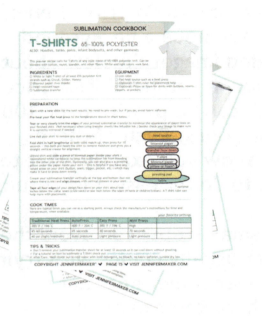

Are you starting sublimation? Can't remember how long to press that sublimation blank? Not sure what order to stack your layers?

The Sublimation Cookbook guide can help, with step-by-step sublimation project recipes for over 150 different sublimation blanks. Each of these "recipes" show you exactly what to use, how long to press, how hot to press it, and how to take care of your sublimated project for long lasting results.

Find out more at
sublimationcookbook.com

CRAFT A LIFE YOU LOVE

Visit me at JenniferMaker.com regularly for inspiration, help, and projects!

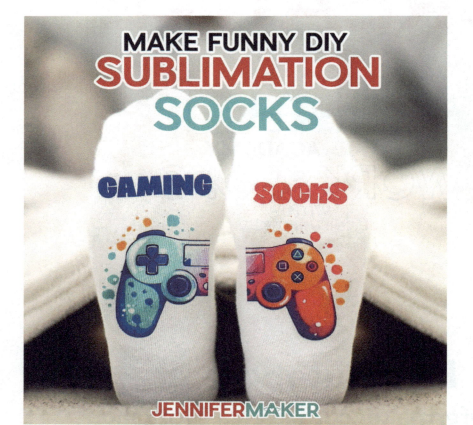

DIY Funny Socks with Sayings — "If You Can Read This, Bring Me..."

Made in the USA
Las Vegas, NV
13 January 2024

84316769R00079